GLOBAL GRACE

God's Ultimate Plan of Salvation for the WHOLE of Mankind

No one is lost, no one. Yes, many have died. But **no one** is in hell. They all sleep waiting for the resurrection to **a Second Physical Life**.

It's taken over 1,500 years to recapture this **lost part of the gospel**.

Read the entire story from beginning to end.

It's what Jesus Christ knew. It's what the Apostles knew.

Now it's time for the **21st century** to re-discover that which was lost . . .

Global Grace

God's Ultimate Plan of Salvation
for the WHOLE of Mankind

JAMES GLOVER

PREMIER PUBLICATIONS

Helensburgh

Unless otherwise indicated, biblical quotations are
from the New King James Version © 1979, 1980, 1982 by
Thomas Nelson Inc., Publishers.

UK ISBN: 978 0 9551605 2 3

First published in the United Kingdom 2012 by
Premier Publications,
P.O. Box 26623, Helensburgh G84 4AH UK

Dedication

A work of this magnitude has not been possible without drawing on the extensive research of the tens of thousands of dedicated scholars who have gone before me.

Men and women from all the major disciplines of academia, science and theology whose own contribution (in some cases, a lifetime's worth) helped produce another link in the chain of unlocking the greatest mysteries of our time.

A special thank you to those who stuck with me during times of extreme stress and self-doubt and to all those who inspired me, a countless number, too numerous to mention.

And let us not forget the Architect that stands behind all this: the risen Christ, the literal embodiment of the hope of all humanity.

Contents

PART ONE

How it All Began . . .

So this is it. We're almost at the end of six thousand years of human history and we're living in a time of culmination. **Some major events lie just ahead of us** and we need to know what is about to happen and how we should prepare for it.

We all started out being born into a world we can barely understand. It's like catching the last five minutes of a two hour movie and then trying to explain to everybody else what it was all about.

No one on Earth can do that. There's no lack of theories and speculations but what we really need is a review of someone **who has seen the whole thing**.

The only source on Earth that claims to have the whole story is the Bible. And what you're about to read is **a summary of the entire Biblical account**, fully deciphered and readily explained using anecdotal evidence from our own lives. These will be things that we're all familiar with. The family, children, health issues, your job, what you eat, sleeping, leisure pursuits, relationships, animals, wars, the weather, nature, the economy, the past, the future, superstition and all aspects of the world in which we live.

YOU SEE, GOD'S PLAN OF SALVATION ISN'T JUST WRITTEN INTO THIS BOOK WE CALL THE BIBLE, IT'S ACTUALLY WRITTEN INTO THE FABRIC OF HIS CREATION, WHAT YOU AND I SEE AROUND US EVERY DAY.

You should be aware that what we think of as **death is not the end, it's just the beginning**. Death is a transition from one consciousness to another and EVERYONE, reading this book, has experienced it. You just don't know it because no one has explained it to you. More on this later . . .

Two thousand years ago, a small group of people were instructed to spread some wonderful news to people all over the Earth.

It wasn't bad news but a fantastic revelation that would gladden the hearts of all who heard it. **Somewhere along the way, that message got corrupted** and has been replaced with threats and fear. That corrupted message has held sway for over fifteen hundred years and it's time to set the record straight.

So here's the whole story, told in the order of events as they actually happened. It takes us up to the present day and also way off into the future . . .

A QUEST FOR TRUTH

Global grace is all about God's ultimate plan of salvation for the whole of mankind. But to be relevant, accurate and truthful; **this account must be able to answer 12 crucial questions** that, up to now, have defied any previous attempt at rational explanation.

These 12 questions are written out below, BUT, I am not going to attempt to answer them or even comment on them, NOT YET. The answers to these Questions will be revealed as we make our way through this story. Then, in the closing stages of this story, we will look at those 12 Questions again and you will be presented with a full and clear answer to each one and all the answers will originate from the Bible itself.

These 12 questions are as follows:

1. Why did God create me
2. If God exists, why does He allow so much suffering?
3. You say there is One God, then how come there are so many religions?
4. I live in a nation where half the people are starving, the crops have failed and civil war is rampant. How will knowing God's plan change this situation?
5. My son was a murderer and ended up committing suicide. Will I ever see him again?
6. I cannot stand injustice, but I know men that have raped, tortured, stolen, cheated and lied and yet they are prospering. Can God explain this?
7. My friend never received Jesus Christ as her personal saviour, but she spent her life helping others. She has since died, has she gone to hell?
8. Eternal life may sound good, but what will we spend eternity doing?
9. When we take the sum total of every man, woman and child that has ever lived, or is living now, we find that less than one in every 200 people, across the world are, or have been, committed Christians. Isn't the devil winning hands-down with less than 1% of the total world population making it into heaven?
10. My sister was sexually abused as a child, put on the street as a prostitute at the age of 12 and is now dying of AIDS and other STDs. How can God help her?
11. The animals, the birds & the fish in the sea haven't done anything wrong, so why do they suffer and do they go to heaven when they die?

12. Disability, illness and disease are a fact of life for millions of people, even today, what can God do for them?

These questions deserve answers and these, **and many other Questions, will be answered**, simply by understanding God's plan for the whole of mankind as revealed in ALL the scriptures and set out chronologically, as it happened.

IN THE BEGINNING

Our story begins BEFORE the creation of Man, BEFORE the creation of our planet, BEFORE the creation of the Universe, BEFORE the creation of the angels. It begins BEFORE the creation of Time and Space. It begins in what the Bible refers to as The Heavenly Realm, a place of permanent existence. **This place does not exist in the Physical dimension** and it remains undetectable by the 5 senses of human beings.

Within this realm dwells the God family, comprising three members: The Bible identifies them as God the Father, God the Son (the one who became Jesus Christ) and God the Holy Spirit. They are Eternal Spirit Beings that have ALWAYS existed and here is where we meet our first problem . . .

How on earth are we supposed to be able to comprehend eternity? As human beings, everyone of us has a birthday. A specific day and time when we came into being. That first moment of consciousness that we celebrate every year. So we find it difficult to comprehend someone who had no beginning. **We have no common frame of reference to aid us in understanding that**. So our perception of God is impaired by being unable to relate to the absolute permanent existence of God.

A DIVINE CONVERSATION

So, at this moment, before creation began, a conversation took place between the members of the God family about **a momentous plan of which you and I are all part**. Now this conversation is something that we can all relate to because there are many of us that have had a very similar conversation. It's when a man and a woman begin discussing the prospect of having a family.

Now it is impossible for me to over-stress this crucial and critical point. GOD WANTS A FAMILY. Not a small family, God doesn't do small. **He wants a gigantic family**, a family of billions upon billions of children.

Look at the size and complexity of the universe with its trillions of stars, planets and suns. Why did He make it? Because He wants a family. He created the angels why? To facilitate His dream of having a family. He created the planet Earth in preparation for His family. Look at the experiences of humanity down through the ages, the accomplishments, the disasters, the joys, the miseries. EVERYTHING and I do mean everything boils down to this basic fact that God wants a family. You cannot understand ANYTHING in the Bible unless this basic fact is burned into your brain, **God wants a family and what God wants, He will have** and NOTHING and I do mean NOTHING will stand in the way of His accomplishing that.

This was the essence of that divine conversation. Now, in human terms, what is the ideal way to start a family? First, there has to be absolute unity expressed between a couple through the ceremony of marriage. Remember, I'm talking about the ideal situation, most of us fall well short of that, but marriage means a rock-solid, life-long commitment between a man and a woman. **This leads to unity of purpose, it leads to unity of love**, to be of one mind and one body and from the security of this relationship, they can discuss the prospect of having children, to create their own family. One boy, one girl? How about three of each? This ideal couple will discuss the TIMING of having children. **They will agree on how they should be raised, what their futures will be and what provision will be made for them**. Well this was the nub of that divine conversation. But as I've already said, God wants a family of billions.

STARTING THE GOD FAMILY

This is the ultimate desire of the God family. They have planned for AND THEY ARE EXECUTING their desire for a family of billions of God children or children of God. Everything has been worked out. **NOTHING has been left to chance**. Everything in the Bible, and I do mean everything, must be read and understood with this crucial element in mind that God desires to have a family and **He has constructed and set up everything to accomplish this**. This is the mind of God, His chief motivation and I'll say this again for emphasis, Nothing and I do mean nothing will stand in the way of this objective being achieved. **All of creation was made for this purpose**, the universe, the angels, this planet, everything. Sin won't stop it, death won't stop it, unbelief won't stop it. **Failure to understand this crucial and critical point will lead to error in everything else**. THIS is our starting point . . . IT'S WHY WE EXIST.

Let's go on. It's important to understand that the Bible reveals to us that the God family are composed of spirit. They are NOT sustained by food or drink, they don't need air to breathe. They don't get hot or cold, get tired or feel physical pain. **They are self-existing**. They are not subject to time and space and they cannot die.

Their power is so great that for us to try and understand it, for us to try and grasp it in our finite minds is like trying to fit a million megatonne nuclear explosion into an eggcup. We just can't comprehend it. We look at the vastness of space, the complexity of our own solar system, the suns, the moons, the planets and the stars and we are left with just a complete sense of awe. **They are in the creation business** but the most awesome fact of all is that their primary motivation behind everything that they do is love.

PERFECT LOVE IS . . .

Now given the world in which we presently live, we really need to take a closer look at what this word love means because its use has been perverted out of all recognition of its original meaning. We have to recognise that **there are three different definitions or contexts to the word love**. The best interpretation of each of these three definitions can be found in the original Greek language:

We start with the definition that most of us are familiar with: EROS, this is the Greek word that defines romantic or sexual love. This definition of love is driven more by the desires of the flesh and the senses than more nobler motives. It can be our greatest source of joy and the root cause of some of our greatest misery.

So how about another Greek word that defines love. What about PHILIA? Loosely translated, this refers to Brotherly love, or kindred spirit. This is often borne of deep friendship, or closeness to siblings or a deep sense of belonging and closeness within a particular group. It tends to be very possessive.

People join gangs and clubs and institutions just to feel part of a particular group. Members of a family can spend all day squabbling amongst themselves until some external threat shows up that puts the whole family in jeopardy. Then they'll come together to repel that threat.

But as soon as peace and safety have been restored we go right back to mutual good-natured animosity. Lots of arguing but still held together by this philial bond of self-interest.

So finally that leaves us with our last Greek word for love. This one is AGAPÉ. The only conceivable way to define the word AGAPÉ is as Godly love. Or **love that is utterly devoid of selfishness**. This is a love that transcends concern for the self. It is sacrificial love where your life is worth less to you than the life of another person, even if that person is a stranger. Even if that person may have done you, or someone you care about, great harm. It is an un-natural love because it does not exist in the human nature of man, it is an alien concept to most human beings.

This love originates only from God, it is perfect love, devoid of ALL jealousy, self-interest and pride. **This love is quick to forgive a wrong and looks only for the best in all people**. And, fortunately, for humanity, as we shall see later, this love defines our God and this motivation governs everything He has done by creating us.

As human beings, especially living in this world, it is difficult for us to grasp the length, breadth and depth of the love that the God family has towards us, especially as **we tend to blame Him for everything going wrong in our lives**, but that's because of deception which we will look at in just a moment. It also hasn't been revealed, until now, what God really had in mind when He created us. So let's continue with this fascinating story . . ..

So God wants children, but what will God's children look like? Well, those of us who are mothers and fathers know that our children have inherited many of our characteristics. They look like us, they have similar features. So what will God's children look like? God is a Spirit Being, so **His children will also be composed of spirit**. He creates, so His children will be imbued with the same creative power. At the moment, however, we are all physical. We are all made from elements that exist only on the earth and the bodies we do have are subject to decay and have a very temporary life span and we will see why shortly.

NO CHOICE BUT FREE-WILL

God is motivated by this extraordinary characteristic of unselfish love, so **His children will be defined in the same way**, BUT there is one other essential element that defines who God is . . . self-will. He is autonomous, free to make His own decisions. **We cannot be like Him unless we're also granted that same freedom of choice**.

Once again, we have to look at our life experience to see what this is like. As parents, the scariest time in the development of our children is when they reach puberty. Why? Because at this time, self awareness (knowledge of self) reaches its peak and with self knowledge comes a sense of independence and self-reliance. Independence of thought and action is seen, by the teenager, as critical to establishment of self-worth. Freedom of choice is hard-wired into the DNA of all human beings. It's the inherent desire of all peoples and nations.

It is this element of choice (self-determination) or doing what YOU want to do that God's children (us) must have to be individual, self-existing, spirit beings. We need our OWN thoughts, our own desires, our own plans and motivation. Without this, we simply become automatons: Robotic creatures enslaved to a specific function, unable to plan or create of our own volition, robbed of the freedom of choice!

EXPERIENCE, NOT CREATION

This critical element of being a child of God could not be created by mere input. **It had to be created by experience** and it had to be done BEFORE we could be trusted with the great and limitless powers of our Heavenly Father. It had to be done BEFORE we could be released into the outer limits of His creation. We have to be able to FREELY choose His perfect, love-motivated ways of doing things rather than **expose His creation to a selfish mindset** that could and would cause great harm to everything He has created.

Again, as parents, I would expect you to understand that. If you have a six-year-old son who comes up to you one day and says "Dad, do you mind if I take the car out tonight?" You wouldn't go along with that, why?

Why wouldn't you give him the use of your car? For a start he's only so high, he hasn't grown up enough yet, **he's not mature enough yet, he's not been trained, he hasn't developed enough**. And if you were so irresponsible as to give your car to a 6-year-old boy, not only could he end up badly injuring other people but he could seriously hurt or even end up killing himself.

So this idea of learning how to take responsibility for our own actions, of **developing character and maturity before we're trusted with greater power** is understood by all of us. Christians, in particular, know that we have to develop our knowledge of God's ways not just by learning about them but by implementing them in our own lives. Only then, through trial and experience can we be trusted with greater blessings and authority to positively impact the lives of others.

You know, we've seen Hollywood movies on this subject: of what it would be like if we developed space travel to the extent that we could start colonising other planets. Wherever we go we take our human nature with us, characterised by greed, selfishness and violence. That won't be permitted. **First, we must deal with our nature**. Once that's been sorted out, then, and only then, will we be endowed with both the means and the opportunity to explore the fulness of God's creation.

So His children, us, humanity, would have to **start out as PHYSICAL human beings** and we would be made to dwell, for a short period of time, on a specially designed testing station, which would be equipped with physical manifestations of the Heavenly Realm that would sustain and challenge all the people living there. We know this testing station as the Planet Earth. Much more on this later.

SUMMARY OF PART ONE

The Bible is a very PRACTICAL book.

The Bible is frighteningly accurate about EVERY subject it covers.

Its warnings should be heeded.

Its claims investigated.

Its advice should be taken seriously.

HOW DO WE DISTINGUISH TRUTH FROM ERROR?

1. The Bible claims 100% accuracy. No errors, no contradictions.
2. The Bible should NEVER be subject to private (man-made) interpretation.
3. The Bible interprets itself.
4. We cannot add or take-away ANYTHING from the scriptures. It is complete.
5. All Bible teachers are held to strict accountability.

God's plans are revealed in scripture like a great big Jigsaw Puzzle.

All the pieces are there but they have to be put together in the right order.

We cannot do that until we know what the finished picture is supposed to look like.

His plans are also revealed in everything He created (Romans 1v20)

HOW DID IT ALL START?

It began with a divine conversation.

A conversation familiar to many of us.

It's when a man and a woman begin discussing the prospect of having a family . . .

God wants a family of BILLIONS of children.

This fact MUST be established in our minds BEFORE we can hope to understand anything else.

God wants a family and NOTHING will be allowed to prevent that from happening.

ALL of Creation was made for THIS purpose:
The Universe.
The Angels.
All life on Earth.
Sin won't stop it. Death won't stop it. Unbelief won't stop it.
THIS IS OUR STARTING POINT. IT'S WHY WE EXIST . . .

God is motivated by Love, but what kind of Love?

AGAPÉ: Sacrificial love. Unselfish love. True Godly love.
An alien concept to many people . . .

WHAT WILL GOD'S CHILDREN BE LIKE?

1. God is a Spirit, so His children will be Spirits.
2. God is a Creator, so His children will be creative.
3. God is motivated by sacrificial love, so His children must have the SAME motivation.
4. God is also autonomous, so His children must be able to exercise that same freedom of choice.
5. We will remain limited and dependent in the physical world until we've dealt with our nature.

PART TWO

The Purpose of Creation . . .

And so, Creation began; but it didn't start with the Earth or the Physical Universe. **Creation began with the Angels**. Unlike human beings, the angels were not created as physical beings but as spirit beings. Nor were they made in the image of God or endorsed as children of God, but rather they were created as the servants of God. **Their primary function was to serve and assist God in all matters pertaining to His great plan**, to have a family.

God loves variety and the angels were created in different forms and endowed with specific functional ability. They were given limited creative power (though far in excess of what humanity has) though they cannot procreate. **Each angel was created as a unique entity** with a different ability, shape, position and level of responsibility and authority from all the others.

It's important to note that there is a divine order to every part of God's creation. In the angelic realm, positions were not earned but conferred at conception. At the top of the tree, so-to-speak, are the Arch-angels. The Bible reveals there are three of them: Gabriel, Michael and Lucifer. Each Arch-angel had authority over one-third of all the angels. They are like the three Generals that command the entire angelic population.

CONSTRUCTING THE UNIVERSE

The next stage of creation was the physical universe. Some scientists subscribe to the Big Bang theory; that order somehow came out of chaos. This is not as far removed from the truth as it may sound. Anyone who has ever been involved in a major, modern-day construction project knows that **you begin with meticulous planning**. Everything is pre-designed to fit into its respective part. Shipping schedules determine precisely when each part must arrive at its assigned position. All form and function is pre-determined.

The various parts, wherever possible, are constructed prior to shipment to the site. **The final stage is assembly where all the parts are placed in their proper order**. This final stage is what most people get to see and it's an awesome sight and they forget the massive preparation that went on prior to implementation of the final stage.

That's why, when we go to watch a 2-hour movie, we have no concept of the thousands upon thousands of man hours, the equipment and costs that went into producing it.

So it just boggles the mind to try and comprehend the level of preparation that went into the creation of the universe, but it all **culminated in the so-called Big Bang** which was the FINAL STAGE of the creation of the Universe, where all the parts flew out at the speed of light until they reached their assigned position where they will remain until God chooses to move them if He so desires.

Is the universe still expanding as many astronomers seem to believe? The answer is probably yes. If you throw a rock into a pond, the ripples don't stop until they reach the shore. The Universe won't stop expanding until it reaches the shores decreed by God and only He knows when that will be.

THE FIRST EARTH

All the planets, created with their suns, moons, stars and solar systems were never-the-less left unfinished. They were certainly not capable of supporting physical life and lacked certain essential ingredients such as water. **But there was one planet that was to receive God's personal attention**. From the power of His Holy Spirit, from which all life is derived, He transformed the planet called Earth from a dry, barren, unfinished globe into a beautiful, lustrous world that was similar to, but completely different from, the world as we know it today. When the angels saw it, they gasped in amazement and praised God when He told them that FOR SOME, this was to be their home in which to use the creative powers He had given them.

One third of all the angels would occupy Earth and it was to be the one-third who were governed by the Arch-angel Lucifer.

Now, the Bible tells us that God NEVER changes the way He does things and one of those things is **He always lets His servants know what He plans to do BEFORE He carries it out**. Inevitably, this meant that at some point He must have called the three Arch-angels together to explain to them why He had created the Earth and the fact that He intended to create billions of direct descendants from God Himself.

Now please don't miss this critical point. Even though the angels are individually created spirit beings, they must, also, have the right of free-will, **(after all, without free-will, no one would be able to rebel)**. This means they would also be subject to testing. For the Arch-angels and all the angels under them, this was their test. **Would they cooperate with God and work with Him to accomplish His purpose of having a family or would they rebel?**

Lucifer was given charge over the angels on the Earth and, for a long period of time, they used their creative powers to create forms of wildlife not seen on the Earth today. It's purely speculation but many of the so-called pre-historic creatures could have come from this time.

ARCH-ANGEL TO ARCH-ENEMY

Although Lucifer had great powers and responsibility, **he secretly desired the Throne of Heaven for himself** and he resented the fact that he would lose his present standing to God's children who would obviously be given pre-eminence over the angels. This created a root of bitterness within him and these jealous thoughts festered. **But how quickly he forgot that without God he wouldn't have the life and privilege he already enjoyed**. But he did forget and this unresolved root of bitterness began to consume him.

So, little by little, he began to communicate his frustrations to the other angels. He began a whispering campaign telling the angels that God was unfair and unjust, that He looked upon the angels as nothing more than slaves for His future children. **He sowed discord and discontent and he didn't quit until he had turned ALL the angels on earth against God**. He made rebels out of all of them. Obviously, he tried to recruit Gabriel and Michael too and all THEIR angels but he didn't succeed.

PROOF OF GOD

Now I want to pause in our story for a moment to make an observation. Over the years I've spoken to many atheists and other unbelievers who mock the idea of the very existence of God. Show me the proof, they say. Where's your evidence? Now I can't summon God to show Himself, just to satisfy their questions. **For each person, there needs to be a personal intervention** that is very rarely a public event and often coming at a time of great personal need to that individual. But in this part of our story, we find that Lucifer has successfully turned one-third of all the angels against God. **Did he do this by claiming God doesn't exist?** No, of course not because all the angels have seen God, they've also seen and probably visited the Heavenly realm. They know God is real, they know God's power, they know what His level of authority is. They have no experience of being oppressed or cruelly treated by God and yet, **in spite of this lack of provocation, Lucifer successfully turned the angels against their Creator.** Now I ask all my readers to consider this: If Lucifer could use his powers of persuasion to turn angels against God, how much of a challenge does humanity represent? **The Bible tells us the whole world has been deceived** and none of us would even realise it unless someone points it out to us and that's what the Bible does . . . but let's go on with our story . . .

WAR IN HEAVEN

God was obviously aware of what was going on and approached Lucifer about his conduct, encouraging him to repent and change his behaviour. But Lucifer lusted after the throne of God, he desired to be like the most High. He wanted to be adored and worshipped by all of creation so, filled with pride, confident there was nothing he couldn't do, **he slowly drew up his plans for the very first coup-d'état.** Eventually the time came and Lucifer, along with all the other rebellious angels, launched a massive attack into the Heavenly Realm. But the attempt was futile, they were repelled by God and sent crashing back to Earth.

The damage, however, was already done. The surface of the Earth was destroyed. **Much of the surrounding cosmos lay in ruins** and the rebellion had finally turned the minds of Lucifer and his angels so that their opposition to God now turned to pure hatred. One third of all the angels had now become demons (REBELS) and Lucifer, in light of his rebellious nature and the fact that he led them, was re-named Satan, which means ADVERSARY or enemy of God.

We should note that God is aware of everything going on in His creation. He knew what Satan was up to and He knew this was going to happen before Lucifer was even created. **Why didn't God stop him before it ever got to this?** Because it was part of the plan. God needed Satan to act as a challenge to His future creation. The angels had a choice about whether to go along with Lucifer or, instead, choose to remain loyal to God. If this was the challenge for the Servants of God (the angels), **how much more of a challenge was going to be needed for the Children of God?** Is the sorry state of the fallen angels permanent? Well, the Bible indicates that the Church will one day be judging angels but how that will work has not yet been revealed.

THE FIRST EARTH IS RUINED

The Planet Earth was in a terrible state (what we refer to as the Ice age) though some Christian teachers allude to this resulting from the great flood but that was impossible as we will soon see. **So God began to get the Earth ready for human habitation** (how He does this is described in the book of Genesis, which is the first book of the Bible).

SUMMARY OF PART TWO

To BECOME children of God, we have to FREELY choose God's perfect, love-motivated ways of doing things, rather than going our OWN way.

This can only be accomplished through EXPERIENCE . . .
A PHYSICAL life experience of CHOICES and CONSEQUENCES.

CREATION BEGAN WITH THE ANGELS

Each angel was created as a unique spirit entity with a different ability, shape, position and level of responsibility and authority from all the others.

Three Arch-angels: Gabriel, Michael and Lucifer, each command one-third of all the other angels.

God NEVER changes the way He does things and one of those things is always to let His servants know what He plans to do BEFORE He carries it out.

To ably assist God, the angels would also need to exercise the right of free-will.
This was their test: Would they cooperate with God and work with Him to accomplish His purpose of creating His family, or would they rebel?

Lucifer was given dominion over the Earth, but He resented God's plan.
Although Lucifer had great powers and responsibility, he secretly desired the Throne of Heaven for himself
He turned ALL the angels on Earth against God and plotted the very FIRST coup d'état.

The Earth and the Cosmos was devastated by this war.
But God restored the Earth and prepared it for human habitation.
Then God created Man.

PART THREE

The Fall of Man

God's creation began with the angels. Under Lucifer, one of the three archangels, one third of the angels turned against God and there was war in Heaven. Those rebellious angels became demons or rebels and Lucifer was re-named as Satan or the adversary, enemy, of God and they were cast back down to Earth.

THE IMAGE OF GOD

Once the Earth had been made ready for human habitation, God formed Man out of the same components with which He had created the Earth **and then placed in Man the spirit of Life**. This also provided him with his mind function (the soul) which gave him the capacity to think, create and feel. All these components that make up a man, the flesh, the soul and the spirit are **interweaved at a sub-atomic level**. God is described as three beings in one: God the Father, God the Son and God the Holy Spirit . . . the Holy Trinity. When He made Man, God said, "Let Us make Man in Our image!" **Man is also a Trinity Being**: Man the Body, Man the Soul and Man the spirit, (the full implications of this are explained in my book *Exposing the Curse*).

Man was created to NEED fellowship with his Creator. **Without that he is incomplete and totally earth-bound in all his perceptions**. He cannot understand spiritual concepts without DIVINE perception.

LIVING IN PARADISE

God named the first man Adam which literally means **Man of the Earth** and placed him in a large park called Eden which means Paradise. God had formed Eden to be the very first dwelling place for Man. **Within its borders Adam was secure.** God's peace rested on this place. Even the animals within these borders were friendly and didn't fear Adam. Everything was provided for him: Trees and plants that yielded delicious fruits, a temperate climate, the relaxing sound of babbling brooks and streams. Everything that Adam could possibly wish for was given to him AND **God appeared everyday, in human form**, to walk with him and teach him directly. Adam saw God physically and interacted with Him physically.

This was an idyllic existence, it was truly paradise. Millionaires today try to re-create this kind of setting in their own way, but they're never really successful and we will see why later on.

Outside the Park of Eden was a wilderness and wild animals roamed feeding on living flesh. It wasn't safe out there but, in the presence of God, as represented by the Garden of Eden, there was both peace, prosperity and safety. Many Bible scholars will disagree with this statement. They will assert that prior to the fall of Man, the whole Earth was a paradise. But they're forgetting that Satan and his demons were consigned to Earth. After Satan attempted his coup-de-ta, he and the demons were cast back down to Earth but he still retained his original dominion over the Earth that God had given him before the rebellion. When God prepared the Earth for human habitation, **He did not banish Satan from it**, so his evil influence was already at work in the Earth.

These scholars also assert that Adam was to have rulership and dominion over the Earth under God and Satan would not be able to influence him. Well yes, that was the plan but **Adam's dominion**

would NOT extend beyond Eden UNTIL he had first been proved or tested. Prior to the outcome of that test, Adam's dominion would NOT extend beyond the borders of Eden. As we know (or as we're soon to find out), Adam failed that test, but had he been successful, the borders of Eden would have been pushed out until eventually Adam's influence (under the guidance of God) would have covered the whole Earth and Satan and his demons would have been permanently ejected.

The fact is: Satan had rulership over the Earth before Adam. Adam was supposed to take over from him but he failed to qualify for that position. He succumbed to temptation and Satan now had dominion over him and consequently ALL OF HUMANITY.

A WIFE FOR LIFE

So let's return to Adam in his pre-fallen state. Man was shown that he had pre-eminence over everything that came into the Garden of Eden. God instructed him to **name the animals, the plants and the trees** just as Man does today, but Adam felt lonely, isolated and incomplete, it was at this point that God created woman. She was created out of the side of Adam to signify her future position in life to be BY his side **to assist him as an equal not as inferior** as some have mistakenly believed. and Adam called her Eve which loosely means Mother of the living. She was presented to Adam as his wife by God and there was a very clear delineation of responsibility. **Man was required to protect, defend, look after and, in every way, love his wife.** His wife was to have pre-eminence in his life over and above everything except his personal relationship with God.

Together they would bear children of every race and nationality to go and populate the Earth. Every human child born to woman has the potential to become an eternal child of God.

When God created Adam and Eve, they were without disabilities or illnesses of any kind. **They were physically and mentally perfect, living in a perfect home and were friends with God who they saw every day.** The One who created them and spoke with them everyday was the Word (the Logos), the very same Being who became Jesus Christ 4,000 years later. During the first 4,000 years, the Bible refers to Him as YAHWEH or, the Eternal One.

THE ETERNITY TEST

As we mentioned earlier, it was necessary for God to begin testing His children.

Let's remind ourselves of the reason behind that. One essential element that defines who God is . . . is self-will. He is autonomous, free to make His own decisions. **We cannot be like Him unless we're granted that same freedom of choice.**

It is this element of self-determination or doing what YOU want to do that God's children (us) must have to be individual, self-existing, spirit beings. We need our OWN thoughts, our own desires, our own plans and motivation.

This critical element of being a child of God could not be created by mere input. It had to be created by experience and it had to be done BEFORE we could be trusted with the great and limitless powers of our Heavenly Father. It had to be done BEFORE we could be released into the outer limits of His creation. We have to be able to **FREELY choose His perfect, love-motivated ways of doing things** rather than expose His creation to a selfish mindset that could and would cause great harm to everything He has created.

So His children would have to start out as PHYSICAL human beings and we would be made to dwell, for a short period of time, on this specially designed testing station, which would be equipped with physical manifestations of the Heavenly Realm that would sustain and challenge all the people living there. We know this testing station as the Planet Earth.

A CHOICE OF WHO TO BELIEVE

So, this is why it was necessary for God to begin testing His children. He told Adam and Eve about a tree in the midst of the Garden called: "The tree of the Knowledge of Good and Evil". He said that they were not to eat the fruit of it under any circumstances, that, if they did, they would DIE that VERY SAME DAY. The tree of Eternal Life was also close by, but it's fruit was not ripe yet.

Now, up to this point, Adam and Eve had only spoken with the Creator and they believed everything He told them without question. **There was no one else offering an alternate point of view**. It's like our personal experiences today. Our children, when they're very young, believe everything their parents tell them, but as they're exposed to other influences, they question more and more what their parents have been teaching them and they're faced with a choice: Do we believe our parents on this issue, or do we believe this other explanation? Now Adam and Eve were about to encounter a different viewpoint, so **who would they believe?** The Creator who had given them everything including life itself, or this stranger who was completely unknown to them?

And so, Satan comes along, disguising himself, taking the form of a serpent and approaches Eve while she is off by herself. He engages her in conversation and, as he did with the angels at an earlier time, **Satan casts aspersions on God's Word** and tempts her with lies and deceit. Convinced by Satan's reasoning, she naïvely takes the fruit, eats some and gives some to her husband (who eats it knowing that he shouldn't). **Instantly, the protective veil of innocence is lost!** What

Adam should have done was wait until the Lord came down in the evening and ask Him about what the serpent had said to his wife. Imagine how different human history would have been if he had just done that.

HUMANITY DIES

Humanity had failed the first critical test, not even putting up a fight and now Adam and Eve were dead.

DEAD? HOW COULD ADAM AND EVE BE DEAD?

The Bible says that Adam went on to live at least 900 years after that day and Eve had lots and lots of children. So how can I say they were now dead?

Because God makes a huge distinction between physical existence (which we all experience, regardless of what we believe) and real abundant, joy-filled, happy, prosperous, healthy lives. **His ways bring life, real life, all other ways result in the hopeless, miserable existence that the Bible calls death**.

Now Adam and Eve realised they were naked. They felt shame and fear. They were now scared of God and hid from Him when He came looking for them in the cool of the evening. MANKIND HAS BEEN HIDING FROM GOD EVER SINCE. They also sewed together fig leaves to cover up their own nakedness. The Lord later replaced these with clothes made from animal skins. The representation is clear. **Humanity cannot cover his own sins** by using fig leaves or anything else. No act of contrition or good acts of any kind can erase the sins of the past. There has to be a blood sacrifice that has to be worth more than the life of the human being who committed these sins. These animals were sacrificed in lieu of the ultimate sacrifice to be made by God Himself.

THE ROT SETS IN

God knew what had happened. His beautiful children were now tainted. Their nature would now represent that of their new father Satan and all the blessings that had been theirs, prior to this failure, would now disappear; including the automatic inheritance of Eternal Life which God so desperately wanted them AND US to have. **Now they, and all humanity onwards, were condemned to die**, never to live again, **to become as if we had never existed**. Adam and Eve, to all intents and purposes, were now dead. They were condemned, without hope, lost and living under a cruel, oppressive, hate-filled regime of demonic influence that would dominate and control their future and the future of all humanity.

WHEN ACCUSATION *IS* ENOUGH

Some argue, this was a terrible price to pay for eating a piece of fruit, but they miss the point. Adam and Eve were given EVERYTHING, they were prohibited from doing just ONE THING. The first person to come along and say something that was contrary to the specific command of God and they heed him rather than go and ask their provider, their sustainer, their best friend, their God. This happens today, ALL OF THE TIME. Someone hints that your wife is having an affair. What happens? You start to believe it. Someone says your parents are drug dealers, your brother is a pimp, your sister is sleeping around, your best friend is a thief. On and on it goes. **Our characters are impugned everyday**. Malicious gossip is a growth industry, it destroys reputations and creates relationship breakdown, mistrust, fear and suspicion. In more extreme circumstances, if left unchecked, **it results in wars between nations**. This lesson has to be learned by all of us: it's better to believe someone who has already demonstrated their love for us than to believe someone who slanders and makes unfulfilled promises.

But God had a plan of redemption, not just for Adam and Eve but **for the whole of humanity**. The cost would be huge, but it was a price that God was willing to pay for the sake of His future family and that plan will become clearer as our story continues.

HUMAN NATURE

By disobeying God, Adam and Eve had committed something the Bible refers to as Sin! The definition of sin must be clearly understood: It is not just a criminal act or a lustful thought, **it is human nature that is naturally hostile to God** and His ways. It seeks only its self-interest, even at the expense of those around him. It will lie, cheat, distort, corrupt, steal, rape, murder, abuse and destroy to get its own way. Human nature is envious, covetous, impatient and hateful and this pretty much sums up the portrait of humanity without God. When Adam sinned, he LOST his desire for fellowship with God and was instead, adopted by his NEW father Satan.

We already know that a child adopts the traits of his father. Humanity has adopted the traits of our earthly father Satan and his **sole motivation is to tempt us toward destruction**. He hates humanity with a vengeance. He views us as pretenders to an inheritance that he believes really belongs to him and **he is completely pre-occupied with our destruction**. Look at Man's legacy since this time: We find what powers the Sun and we make bombs of it. We create wealth and become obsessed with greed, we achieve power and we go mad. Whatever one man seeks to build, another will come and destroy. **Human history is littered with catastrophe**. What starts as a family squabble or political sleight turns into a license for authorised murder. We are all the devil's children, each playing a part in a macabre game that can only end in destruction. From that first fateful day when he tempted our parents to sin, Satan has used his influence to keep us separated from God and at war with each other.

WHEN CHILDREN BECOME ORPHANS

All those blessings that belonged to Adam and Eve, while they remained under God's protection, were lost on that day. Since then, every evil act, illness and cataclysmic event of human history can be traced back to this one supreme truth, "MAN WITHOUT GOD IS LOST!" because it lies within our nature to destroy ourselves and each other.

When God confronted Adam and Eve about what had happened, He also spelled out the consequences. They were both now living under a curse and this curse has followed humanity down through the ages. Cut off from God, Man has used his own wisdom and his own ideas about what should constitute the ideal society and every attempt we have made has failed for one reason or another. Because no nation has ever adopted the perfect laws of God in their entirety and, even when they have (as in the case of ancient Israel) the tempter has always been around to throw a spanner in the works.

Much more on this subject can be found in my book: *Exposing the Curse*.

SUMMARY OF PART THREE

The Earth and the cosmos had been destroyed by this great war.
The Genesis account describes the renovation of the planet Earth to make it fit for human habitation
God created the very first man called Adam and placed him in a beautiful location called Eden which literally means Paradise.

Every human child born to woman has the potential to become an eternal child of God.

We have to be able to FREELY choose His perfect, love-motivated ways of doing things rather than expose His creation to a selfish mindset that could and would cause great harm to everything He has created.

God makes a huge distinction between physical existence (which we all experience, regardless of what we believe) and real abundant, joy-filled, happy, prosperous, healthy lives. His ways bring life, all other ways bring death.

Human nature would now represent that of their new father Satan and all the blessings that had been theirs, prior to this failure, would now disappear; including the automatic inheritance of Eternal Life.

God had a plan of redemption, not just for Adam and Eve but for the whole of humanity.

S.I.N. = Self, Indulgent, Narcissism . . .

Satan is completely pre-occupied with our destruction.

PART FOUR

The Law of Consequences

Now we ended the last part by looking at some of the consequences of sin and how the Bible makes a very clear distinction between physical existence (which we all experience) and real life which is a God-led, abundant, joy-filled, happy and healthy life. **The Bible uses the term SHEOL and HADES (which is sometimes translated as the grave or hell) to describe human existence without God.** In fact, God refers to human existence WITHOUT HIM, as Death or being dead.

When God said to the ancient nation of Israel, "Keep my commandments so that you and your descendants may live." **He wasn't saying that they would all suddenly die if they didn't;** He was indicating that their time on Earth would be a much happier one if they did keep His commandments. They would enjoy real life, abundance and happiness, protection from their enemies and good health. OUR CHOICES DETERMINE OUR FUTURE . . .

THE TORMENT OF SIN

However, if they chose to ignore those commandments, **the consequences for themselves, for their families and children would be catastrophic.** Their harvest would start to fail, illness would increase, now as I start to go through this, I want you to think about the kinds of problems that many nations are experiencing at this time, even our own nation here in the UK. I'll start this point again: Their harvest would start to fail, illness would increase, look at the burden on our National Health Service today, just in the UK. The burden has almost doubled in 10 years but our population hasn't, we can't blame that on an increase in population.

People are getting sicker and sicker and there's more strains and new varieties of viruses, the things we used to be able to protect ourselves against with immunisation and vaccines but we're now finding are meta-morphosizing into superbugs, why? **Because we cannot subvert the way the law works . . . we can't!**

So failing harvests, ill health and violence in their society would also start increasing, families would break down, their enemies would flourish until finally they would be taken into captivity and suffer the most appalling cruelty. Yet **they would still be alive, but they would be dead inside**.

DYING TO LIVE

In most countries, if the father leaves the wife and children to fend for themselves, the consequence is normally exposure to danger, descent into poverty and finally poor health and early death. In the West and most developed countries we have welfare safety nets to help those left in circumstances like this. Now that's a good thing and one of the reasons why the West has been allowed to prosper is because we've made a point of **looking after the poor and disadvantaged among us**. But the analogy still stands; God is our Spiritual Father, while we remain separated from Him and ignore His way of doing things, we expose ourselves to all manner of difficulties and danger. When Jesus was asked by one of his disciples if he could go and bury his father, He said, **"Let the dead bury their own dead"**. From Gods' perspective, human beings who are detached from their Creator by disobedience, outright rejection or even through just sheer ignorance are dead. **Spiritual zombies; alive in their bodies but dead in their spirit**.

Why do people get high on alcohol and drugs?

Why do we pursue high risk activities that result in illness, accidents and early death?

Why are we so incredibly self-destructive in what we think, say and do?

How can we be so accomplished, successful and happy one day and ready to jump under a bus the next?

What makes us so fearful of doing the right things, over which we should have control and so reckless and cavalier when it comes to doing the wrong things that we know will cause us harm?

WHEN OUR SPIRIT ISN'T WILLING

Because, when Adam sinned, he (along with all future human beings) lost his desire for fellowship with God. He lost that desire to maintain a relationship with his Creator. THAT DESIRE TO COMMUNICATE WITH GOD DOES NOT EXIST WITHIN MOST PEOPLE. When most people hear about God they don't have a sudden desire to go before God and start believing and doing what He says and seeing things improve for themselves. **The desire just isn't there, it's the opposite. They feel enmity**. They feel inexplicable feelings of animosity and they can't even really explain these feelings, either to themselves or each other.

Now that desire may not be there but the emptiness is. Some people refer to it as a God-shaped hole in our spirit and we're desperate to fill it. **We will do and try anything to fill it** but nothing will truly satisfy the human spirit until he is re-connected with his Creator.

You see the whole of humanity lives under this destructive influence that emanates from Satan.

He's been depicted in cartoons with horns, hooves and a tail. Different religions refer to him as a shadowy, frightening depiction of an ugly, evil, man-like creature. All these descriptions are illustrative of our over-worked, superstitious imagination. The truth is; **no one has ever seen him**. He hates exposure, but his influence is all around us.

INFANT WARFARE

This process of influencing our nature begins at birth. Every human being is subject to this influence and grows up with it. How many mothers can testify to the so-called "terrible twos" when a young infant begins to test the boundaries placed on him by his parents. Good parents know the importance of appropriate correction when dealing with a wayward child and, if coupled with wise education and **a good example** by the parents, that child can be kept from the worst excesses of his human nature.

However, failure to properly discipline, instruct and mentor that child can and will be ruinous for that child's' future. He/she will grow up exercising little, if any, restraint and will fall into ever greater depths of depravity and personal despair. WRONG CHOICES LEAVE A TERRIBLE LEGACY FOR OUR CHILDREN. But it doesn't end there. If they also end up having children, **their history and the consequences of their past actions will also fall onto their children** and that cycle will continue until the third or fourth generation of that family line until some of the lessons of this life have finally been learned.

Now, these are called generational curses. We have genetic scientists now who have confirmed this and there's no argument. **There's**

no disparity between what science is discovering, good genuine science, and what the Bible has said all along. It's just confirming, if we had read the Bible, what we already know.

CHOICES DEFINE OUR FUTURE

So the Bible tells us we have a choice, or do we? We know we cannot choose our parents. We know we cannot choose the time and location of our birth. We know we cannot choose our siblings and wider family members, so where is this choice? Well **we do have this thing called: "Free moral agency" or "Freedom of choice when making decisions or responding to events"**. Some of our most compelling stories come from people who are born into the worst kind of situations and then make a success of their lives in spite of their desperate circumstances. These people made WISE choices that led them toward good health, successful relationships and prosperity. They got to know about these choices either by accident or through education and **then had the motivation to make the right choice**. Most of us don't make the right choices.

Instead, we find ourselves led astray by lust, greed, envy, laziness, wrath, gluttony and pride; commonly referred to as the seven deadly sins or: A more accurate definition would be to describe these seven deadly sins as **the traits or motivational force of our fallen nature**.

These traits motivate us or drive us to commit sin. These sins can be lying, stealing, sexual immorality (any sexual act that takes place outside of marriage), cursing, injury to or murder of another with intent, along with many, many others. It's just who we are but there are degrees of offense. An employee who steals a pencil from his employer will not cause the collapse of the Company, but would that same person think twice about raiding the Company's pension fund to finance his own lavish lifestyle and change the rules of the Company to enable him to do it? He probably wouldn't hesitate because the same motivation for stealing a pencil indicates a propensity for dishonesty that, if left unchecked, would lead to embezzlement and theft on a grand scale.

Now what does that remind you of?

What happened a few years ago?

LAWS OR FLAWS

The Crash of Lehman Brothers, the banking system . . . almost the entire banking system of the West came close to a complete collapse. Governments had to put taxpayers under huge debt burdens in order to rescue the banks, to stop the whole system from collapsing and what were the traits of human nature that led to that?

Greed! Wanting something for nothing. Selfishness! That's what occupied the minds of those who changed the rules, and often did it legally.

Too often, **laws are used to benefit a small number of people** in a particular country and when that happens, the majority end up paying the price for it.

Now we've ended up with national debts that are completely unsustainable. Crippling interest rates, austerity measures that are suffocating growth, inflation, high unemployment. These are all the results of poor choices made by individuals and nations.

Is there a way out? Can these nations return to prosperity? Actually, they can.

THE CANAAN PRINCIPLE

The Bible is a very practical book that has the answers to all of life's problems and there is something in the Bible that I like to call the "Canaan Principle".

It's not very well known but if these practical measures were implemented, we would see unemployment almost wiped out within 3 years. We would see extraordinary growth and it wouldn't cost the Governments anything to implement it. All they'd have to do is make some changes in their legislation and re-prioritise some of their tax and spend policies.

But **the real beauty of the Canaan principle is that it could be implemented in any nation on Earth** and the results would always be the same. Prosperity doesn't happen by accident, it's the result of wise choices made by people that are willing to defer to scriptural insight to inspire their decisions.

The banking crisis was a man-made phenomenon brought about by personal ambition, greed and selfishness on the part of people from all walks of life.

HELL *IS* ON EARTH

It's these **motivational traits** that cause us to wander down that broad path to our own destruction and the destruction of those round about us. We end up in prison, broke, homeless, sick, addicted, depressed. Or, we could end up rich, powerful and totally insane, **completely oblivious to the welfare of others**. Then we become hateful, proud, cruel and vindictive, carrying out acts of such depravity that we inspire fear and terror in others that, in turn, start wars and all the misery, famine, disease and pain that emanate from that.

That's our world ladies and gentleman. **This is our SHEOL, our HADES and everyone of us, to a greater or lesser degree, is responsible for it.**

It's this life that the Bible describes as death: living death, or, the way of death. In the West we have worked so hard to alleviate some of the worst effects of this way of life, but it's a losing battle because those motivations, we were talking about earlier, just keep getting stronger and stronger.

We can medicate most forms of illness, sickness and disability but **rarely cure them completely** and even when we do it just becomes a stepping stone to yet another problem. As I mentioned earlier, human beings are one part physical body, one part soul and one part spirit. **If there is a problem in our spiritual self it is manifested in our flesh.**

As human beings we concentrate on curing the flesh but that's not how Jesus did it. **Jesus healed people by forgiving their sins.** Disabilities, mental problems, sickness, disease, paralysis, all were cured with a word from the Creator.

Even the disciples were granted that power and, by extension, the Church. Do you ever think it strange how few people will go to a church Pastor, Priest or Minister to be healed of an ailment? **The most common reason given is that it never seems to work.** Well, the Bible says it does work, but only in a certain way and if the Pastor, Priest or Minister is not familiar with that way then obviously he will be unable to help. I hope that people reading this will get a copy of my book: *Miraculous Healing for the Church* as we reveal in this book the full healing process identified in the Bible.

DIAGNOSING SIN

Ever visited a Doctor and heard him say, "If you don't change your ways you're going to wind up worse than ever or even dead,". The Doctor's warning may be justified but what will he say when the patient asks him **what part of my life do I need to change?** The Doctor may be skilled in medical care but he is not qualified to judge the life of any one individual.

Every time we think we have a handle on the cause behind a medical problem, we always find anomalies. People get sick when they shouldn't, other people, who ignore medical advice, stay robustly healthy. Some patients respond to treatment, others don't. Look at viral infections that are spread either by touch or are air-borne. It's just not true to say that it affects everybody. Some people who come into close proximity with the disease are immune to its effects. Is this some kind of lottery? Is this luck, chance, random acts of good or bad fortune? Let's not get superstitious. Let's not go down that road. Let's be practical.

If you visit a doctor and you have a symptom that is not clearly identifiable, **the doctor will take you through a series of tests and examinations to determine the precise cause of your distress**. In doing so, he may have to ask you very personal questions about your lifestyle and your habits. Let's be honest, this can be embarrassing, even painful but we all agree that this kind of examination is necessary to form an accurate diagnosis of the problem.

Well, **the Bible does this as well, only it goes much deeper** and is much more revealing than a medical examination. The recommended treatment will always involve a lifestyle change, a change in attitude, a change in habits, even a change in the way we think, but **the treatment always works**. No pills, no operations but a steady application of a new way of life that will lead to good health and a peaceful state of mind. We can still avail ourselves of medical treatment if we want to but **it shouldn't replace the healing process identified in the Word of God.**

PARADISE LOST

But let's get back to our story: ADAM & EVE WERE NOW BANISHED FROM EDEN.

So Adam and Eve were now going to have to learn to fend for themselves. They had many sons and daughters who married each other and, who in turn, also bore children of their own. As the family grew big they drifted off into their own groups and built cities to protect themselves from the dangers of the wilderness.

Human nature was tragically manifested very early on with the first recorded murder and sin multiplied with each new generation.

In spite of everything that had happened, **God deeply desired that His children should be reconciled to Him** and the plan to accomplish that began to take shape about 2,000 years after the fall in Eden.

But first, an event of truly Biblical proportions took place around 1,500 years after Eden.

Mankind was well on his way to self-destruction at this time. The Bible declares the WHOLE EARTH was filled with violence, much worse than it is even today. Now this is talking about pre-flood times.

This world-wide flood is known as a great event in Biblical history and for the most part it has been proven by scientific and archaeological research but what is rarely understood is **what was it about humanity and the way they were living that could have caused God to supernaturally flood the entire Earth and kill everyone on Earth who was alive at that time?** And not just all human beings, but animals as well.

AS IN THE DAYS OF NOAH . . .

Well the Bible makes reference to something that was going on within the human experience back at that time that is, even in today's world, with all its moral upsets and moral confusion, is still regarded as something that is deeply offensive and involves actions that people do not want to participate in.

The Bible is referring to events that were going on where there was literally intercourse taking place between humans and animals and where intercourse was taking place between a man and a female animal, the animal was then giving birth to some kind of weird hybrid and if sex was taking place between a woman and a male animal then she would be allowed to become pregnant and she would give birth to a weird hybrid creature and this was common-place right around the world.

Now there were many other evil things going on as well at this time but **the Bible reveals that this particular level of debauchery was the final straw that always preceded divine judgement**. It was creating a tremendous amount of suffering, to the hybrids themselves as well as to others, and it was also leading to extreme aspects of violence.

Why were the people behaving in this way?

Well, one of the reasons was the desire for military advantage. If one group was able to create a vicious super-strong hybrid that could be used to conquer and destroy their enemies, they could guarantee peace and protection to their people and then take over the lands and possessions of others. So they arranged this swap-over of species to try and create a hybrid creature that could defeat all their enemies. Giants forinstance were never the result of natural human relationships, they were the by-product of un-natural couplings between man and beast. One famous Biblical character is Goliath whose physical dimensions were completely unnatural.

HUMAN REASON FOR A SEASON

Supplanting natural laws to meet the needs of human reasoning always brings undesirable consequences.

This co-mingling of human seed and animal eggs, or animal seed and human eggs, and the hybrids that resulted from it, created all manner of weird kinds of disease and led to a huge amount of suffering and this was endemic throughout the world.

Now the only reason why I'm mentioning this is because in today's world that sort of thing is beginning to proliferate our culture in certain pornographic situations. It's often shown as an alternative means of relationship between humans and animals. Obviously, this is completely wrong and extremely dangerous but this practice is referred to by psychologists as zoophilia and also as bestialism which basically means to mate with a beast and unfortunately that is happening more and more but there is something else going on in today's world that you need to be aware of:

There is scientific experimentation going on today where human embryos are being tested and examined to determine whether parts of them can be used to deal with diseases like altzhiemers. They are taking these fertilised eggs and they are changing the genetic structure to try and create new biological solutions to some of man's most intractable problems and then they're basically just standing back to see what happens.

SUMMARY OF PART FOUR

God refers to human existence, WITHOUT HIM, as Death or being dead.

OUR CHOICES DETERMINE OUR FUTURE

RIGHT CHOICES LEAD TO A HAPPY HEALTHY LIFE.

HUMAN BEINGS WHO SEPARATE THEMSELVES FROM THEIR CREATOR BY DISOBEDIENCE, REJECTION OR IGNORANCE ARE DEAD IN THEIR SPIRIT.

THAT DESIRE TO COMMUNICATE WITH GOD DOES NOT EXIST WITHIN MOST PEOPLE.

WRONG CHOICES LEAVE A TERRIBLE LEGACY FOR OUR CHILDREN.

RIGHT CHOICES BRING GOOD OUTCOMES.

THE BIBLE HAS PRACTICAL ANSWERS TO ALL OF LIFE'S PROBLEMS, including THE CANAAN SOLUTION.

It's this life that Jesus described as death: living death, or, the way of death.

God makes a huge distinction between physical existence (which we all experience, regardless of what we believe) and real abundant, joy-filled, happy, prosperous, healthy lives.

HIS WAYS BRING LIFE, all other ways bring death.

HUMAN BEINGS ARE ONE PART PHYSICAL BODY, ONE PART

SOUL (your mind function) AND ONE PART SPIRIT.

JESUS HEALED PEOPLE BY FORGIVING THEIR SINS.

SHOULD WE CURE THE CONSEQUENCE OR THE CAUSE?

See: *Miraculous Healing for the Church*.

THE BIBLE TELLS US THERE IS A LIMIT TO WHAT GOD WILL ALLOW IN HUMAN AFFAIRS BEFORE HE ENACTS FINAL JUDGEMENT.

Supplanting natural laws to meet the needs of human reasoning always brings undesirable consequences.

PART FIVE

The Route to Redemption

We concluded part 4 by examining the state of mankind just prior to the Great Flood. Because sin had proliferated, man was now mixing his seed with animals, producing strange hybrids. **The demonic influence that preceded this activity relates to a section of the fallen angels known as the Nephilim or Rephaim.**

Some scholars have mistakenly assumed that fallen angels mated with humans but Jesus Himself quashed that "error-in-thinking", in His statement in the gospels.

We also contrasted pre-flood times with present-day reality. Bestiality and zoophilia are on the increase as is experimentation with the mixing of species.

Now, I'm well aware that in the West we have passed legislation such as the embryology bill that forbids this kind of experimentation but there are other countries in the world who don't have these restrictions.

So, like it or not, the very conditions that pre-empted divine judgement 1500 years after Eden, which is about 4 and a half thousand years ago, is happening again today in our lifetime.

And this research is not just restricted to human embryos, there are many hybrids of animals that have been formed by crossing species just to see if they can create some new antidote to an illness or create new kinds of food.

They're changing our plant-life too by trying to increase the harvest of crops by changing the genetic structure to increase the yield or to make them resistant to disease or slow down natural decay to increase their shelf-life. Now the idea behind it primarily is so that they can feed more people, now that's a noble motive, there's nothing wrong with wanting to feed more people or to make food cheaper or more available but the trouble is, **if it has an unintended consequence within nature, within natural laws, that are very finely balanced, then we're going to find ourselves dealing with problems that no scientist no physicist no chemist no biologist has been able to foresee**.

We're already starting to see things like anti-biotic resistant strains of disease appearing. There are hospitals and medical labs throughout the world that are conducting research trying to find out what it is that created this new strain that is resistant to antibiotics and they don't yet have all the answers but they're starting to recognise that where they've used certain kinds of drugs and medicine to deal with people's suffering, to try to extend people's lives, all of which are noble motives, **they're having an unintended consequence** and its causing increasing problems and, as I was saying, these events are tied very closely to what was going on four and a half thousand years ago.

So disease, violence, horrible experimentation, **the utter perversion of His creation and the absolute total rejection of His ways, brought the divine judgement that caused God to flood the Earth**. Remember, He didn't just kill every human being when he flooded the Earth, He also took out the animals as well.

We know from our world history that when human society starts going down-hill, it always follows the same path. **Deviancy escalates** until things like bestiality and even cannibalism become common-place . . .

STARTING OVER

So, God supernaturally flooded the whole Earth, killing every living being, **except for the family of Noah who was the only one living a life of peace and concern for his fellow man, out of a good conscience toward God**. God inspired him to build a large boat (an ark) that would house him, his family and the male and female of every kind of animal on Earth to ensure their survival.

So, our lineage traces back to Noah and his family. As with Adam and Eve's children; brother married sister until sufficient generations had passed to allow spouses to be chosen from more distant relatives. All the nations of the Earth came from Noah's family and, in that respect, **we are all related**.

In His promise to never flood the whole Earth again, God set a rainbow in the sky which can be seen when both Sun and Rain mix in every Country on the Planet.

Whenever you see a heavy shower of rain where there's a lot of cloud in one part of the sky and the rest of the sky is clear so the sun is able to come through, a prism effect is made possible and anyone who studies physics will tell you that whenever you shine white light through a prism you get to see all the colours of the rainbow.

But the one thing that physicists have never been able to figure out is **what forms the bow**. They know how the colours come out but they cannot understand why it always comes in the form of a bow and to this day they still haven't been able to figure it out.

But God set a rainbow in the sky as a promise to us and a reminder to Himself, that He would never flood the Whole Earth again.

WHERE EDEN IS TODAY

The Garden of Eden was a literal, physical place that existed on the Earth and had its own geographical location. In pre-flood times its borders were protected and guarded and no human being was ever allowed access to it.

However, after the flood, its existence disappears from Biblical history, but not its geographical location, that would have to remain constant. We must also remember that the flood would have caused topographical changes, causing the relocation of lakes, rivers and streams. So trying to marry the Genesis description of Eden to current locations is pointless because they don't exist anymore. Man may not know where Eden was located but God has not forgotten.

We should not be surprised that God would deliberately focus huge global, life-changing events into one particular area of real estate on the Earth. He, God, chose the Land of Canaan for Israel. He chose the City of Jerusalem for the Temple and for the focal point of Christ's crucifixion.

Even today, every religion seeks a claim on Jerusalem and recent genetic studies, seeking to trace the genealogy of Man's roots, are all being pulled toward the Middle East. Even written languages appear to flow from their country of origin back toward Jerusalem.

Prophecy tells us that in the culmination of the next war, all the nations will send their armies against Jerusalem in order to fight against Jesus Christ when He returns to Earth to set up His Kingdom. And **Jerusalem will be the official Capital city of the entire Earth** when Christ will rule from there over the entire world after His return.

Why is this patch of land so significant? Because it's the geographical location of the original Garden of Eden. It's where the human story began and that's where it will finish.

THE ORIGIN OF LANGUAGES

Approximately 1,000 years after the flood, mankind had again proliferated and was now embarking on major projects. One of these was to build a tower of colossal dimensions that would reach beyond the Earth's atmosphere. **Man, with each generation, was learning at an exponential rate.** Archaeologists have discovered evidence that electrical power had begun to be harnessed at this time and God was well aware that if He didn't intervene, Man would reach a high level of scientific know-how 3,000 years sooner than His original plan allowed.

The main reason behind this explosion of knowledge was the fact that EVERYBODY SPOKE THE SAME LANGUAGE. So communication among the top scientists of the day was unimpaired and **ideas and new discoveries were easily shared**. So, to maintain the time-frame that He had decreed from the outset, God decided to confuse their language!

One language now became fifty and all projects were abandoned as the people congregated into groups that shared their language and thus, **new nations were born.** This inevitably led to a proliferation of different cultures, taboos, customs and mind-sets that made it easier for nations to misunderstand each other, take offense and start wars.

Today, much of that has been alleviated by the use of Embassies, diplomats and consulates. **One universal language, however, did remain and that was the language of numbers and the laws of mathematics.** But it was to be many years before Man could harness the technology to re-establish global communication in the way we have it today.

From this point on in the Bible, global events are largely pushed to one side as the Author concentrates on individuals that God has chosen to work with as He seeks to bring about His plan of redemption.

THE JOURNEY TO REDEMPTION

A man called Abraham is selected by God to be the founding father of what is to become a great nation. He had two sons Isaac and Ishmael. Ishmael was born to a woman called Hagar who was the maidservant of his wife Sarah and was the first-born of Abraham's family but Isaac was born to Abraham's wife Sarah and therefore endowed with Abraham's inheritance rather than Ishmael.

This event is significant because the sibling rivalry that occurred as a result of this event is still played out today among the descendants of Ishmael who are predominantly Muslim and the descendants of Isaac who are predominantly secular, Christians and Jews of the West. **There have been clashes between East and West ever since.** It should be noted by prophecy pundits that the final compilation of the global government currently being assembled will comprise 5 major leaders from the west and 5 major leaders from the East. The world will be divided up between them.

The Bible now concentrates on Isaac's lineage. His wife Rebecca had twin sons: Esau and Jacob. Again, the birthright should have gone to Esau but Jacob contrived to supplant his brother and took the birthright for himself. Later, God changes Jacob's name to Israel which literally means – someone who contends or wrestles with God.

Jacob went on to have 12 sons who became the founding fathers of 12 tribes that grew into great nations but the birthright lineage was to have one more major transition. Joseph was the second youngest of all his brethren and he had two sons called Ephraim and Manasseh. **Unusually, Jacob, their grandfather, decided to adopt Ephraim**

and Manasseh as his OWN sons. This meant that they had equal preference for the birthright blessings that were accorded to Joseph their father.

THE ORIGINS OF THE WEST

Now, why is this significant? Because prophetic assertions about the very times in which we live today cannot be properly understood unless the descendants of Ephraim and Manasseh are clearly identified in our present-day world. This is a highly contentious issue but we cannot possibly hope to comprehend world events and where they are leading unless we accept what the Bible makes abundantly clear to those who have studied these things. **The modern-day descendants of Ephraim are the United Kingdom of Great Britain, the Commonwealth and principalities of the UK. The modern-day descendants of Manasseh are the United States of America and her principalities.**

These facts will be ferociously disputed but those scholars who study history and understand prophecy and are aware of the principles of Biblical interpretation will have no option except to come to the same conclusion.

The modern-day descendants of the other tribes make up the rest of what we refer to as the Western nations; including most of Europe. But it's the English-speaking nations that have had the greatest world influence over the last 300 years and deservedly earn the sobriquet of "Nations-of-Promise" that derives from the birthright conferred upon the descendants of Ephraim and Manasseh. It should be noted that the "modern" State of Israel is made up of predominantly Jewish people and represents only a fraction of the ancient nation from which they derive their name. However, their status in terms of Biblical prophecy cannot be understated.

A CHOSEN NATION

Now the Bible story concentrates on the nation of Israel as it is through their experiences that **God demonstrates the impossibility of Man trying to live his life in complete obedience to God's laws**. He demonstrated through Israel that obedience would bring great blessings including good health, national prosperity, protection from their enemies and happy relationships within their family and with their neighbour. But disobedience would always result in the opposite, bringing calamity, misery, anxiety, oppression and despair.

God's revelation to Israel began with the ten commandments. **A set of instructions upon which a whole society could be founded**. These commandments emphasized the importance of placing God first in both an individual's life and in the national conscience. These commandments also go on to lay the foundation for successful human interaction, for mutual respect and concern for one another. **Any nation that adopts this will flourish. Any nation that rejects them will disintegrate**.

In addition to these commandments, Israel was also given various ordinances that dealt with situations that would come up from time to time, along with judgements, rulings and detailed instructions on how to deal with those who disobeyed. **It is worthwhile to note that many readers of the Old Testament are put off by what is seen as harsh punishment for those who broke the law**. In many cases the punishment was death and, in most societies today, that punishment is only incurred as a last resort, but that is fallible thinking. In almost every case where death was prescribed for those who broke the law, God states unequivocally that the purpose for the death sentence was: "TO PUT AWAY THE EVIL FROM AMONG YOU". In other words, permanent removal of a man who promotes evil, so that the wider society can prosper without straying and the people are protected. Now I go into this subject in a lot more detail in my book *Exposing the*

Curse which deals with all aspects of the premature termination of a human life including murder, suicide, execution and euthanasia.

The reason why "liberal-minded" people are horrified at this prospect of execution of ANYONE is because they see death as permanent, but this is not the case as we shall soon see.

MURDEROUS INTENTIONS

It would be helpful to review the crime of murder at this stage. The Biblical definition of murder is the taking of another person's life with malice afore-thought. According to God, **everyone has been guilty of murder at some point in their lives** because the motive for murder begins in the heart and the motive for murder is hatred. The physical act of murder is merely the outward expression of what was already in the heart, so anyone who preaches hatred against another individual or nation is actually preaching incitement to murder. **Hatred, regardless of cause, is an act of murder that hasn't happened yet**. But God who is able to see both the thoughts and intents of the heart, has already condemned that individual, through the law, because he aspires to murder and **whatever is conceived in the mind will eventually come to pass** unless that mind is changed.

God never hated these individuals, He hated what they did but not who they were. By removing them from this life, He protected them, their loved ones, their victims and wider society by preventing them from doing any further harm. **Execution satisfied the law and no further judgement would be brought on that wider society**. Unfortunately, today, we disregard these instructions. We believe we're more enlightened and, as a consequence, wider society is moving further and further away from God and the seeds of destruction are deeply sown. This is why we have so many genetic abnormalities because the original cause of judgement, that was sown into the life of an individual who has committed a grievous act, is still alive and well through their progeny; through the children that they ultimately have. **It's a legacy of illness, addictions, deformity, mental illness, psychosis and all manner of behavioural problems**. Some Bible students challenge this by referring to scriptures that appear to de-bunk this assertion, but, as in so many areas of misunderstanding, they apply their preconceived logic to a personal interpretation of scripture that makes the Bible look confused and contradictory in its message. But their interpretation is mis-guided not just in trying to understand the Bible but also in terms of real-life experience and genuine scientific discovery on the laws of genetics. Again, I must encourage you to get our book "EXPOSING THE CURSE" to understand precisely how these relational, planet-wide laws actually work.

A RITUAL-BASED COVENANT

It was never going to be possible for carnal-natured man to keep all these laws, commandments, statutes and judgements according to the standard of perfection demanded by God. So **God instituted a program of rituals**, which would fore-shadow future events, to cleanse them of wrong-doing. Remember that humanity had been cut off from God because of Man's sinful nature, so animal sacrifices had to be made on a daily basis as a reminder to Israel of their sinful condition. God was prepared to accept these animal sacrifices as an atonement for the sins of the people in lieu of a much bigger sacrifice by God Himself in the not too distant future. **These rituals enabled Israel to have a relationship with God and formed the basis of the covenant between God and Israel but it excluded anyone else**.

All the other nations were still under the consequences of the law but they couldn't participate in these rituals that would have brought them redemption and healing when they were suffering themselves. But God always intended that Israel would be both a witness and a blessing to other nations. So when they witnessed Israel prospering and enjoying good health, they could send their emissaries to

Israel and learn from them and adopt some of the practices in their own nations and Israel was obligated to teach them. And if a nation conveyed gifts and honour to Israel, **God would accept this as honour toward Himself** and deliberately bless the nation that behaved in this way. Of course, it worked the other way too. If a nation demonstrated hatred toward Israel, they were assuring their own destruction.

CELEBRATING THE FUTURE

Although there were many occasions when Israel slipped up, **God was always willing to forgive them when they repented and went back to keeping the law** which also included the observance of "special days"! These "Holy Days" and "Feasts" were very much a part of the Old Covenant relationship between Israel and God but they also fore-shadowed future prophetic events. **Within these Special Days were laid the foundation of God's redemptive plan for the WHOLE OF MANKIND.** It's kind of like: we all have a birthday but can you imagine your parents knowing the day that you're going to be born long before it ever happens?

For instance, let's say that your parents know you're going to be born on the 10th of January, say, 5 years from now and they know this as a fact. So your parents start celebrating your birthday BEFORE it actually happens. So in the 5 years before your actual birthday, on the 10th of January of each year they throw a little party celebrating the fact that you will soon be coming along. Well that's effectively what was happening here. God had set up Holy Days and Feasts that were foreshadowing events that were yet to happen and the people were commanded to celebrate them but they weren't celebrating something that had already happened, **they were celebrating something that was going TO happen.** By doing this they actually kept the knowledge of these yet-future events in the fore-front of their minds and that's the reason why God established this system within the nation of Israel.

Within these SPECIAL DAYS were laid out God's redemptive plan for the Whole of Mankind.

WHEN HOLY-DAYS
(HOLIDAYS) WERE MORE THAN A VACATION

The Laws, ritual observances and Holy Days all served to distinguish Israel from all the other nations. One in particular was widely known to be associated with Israel and that was their observance of the Sabbath, or the last day of the week (Saturday). **The Sabbath was the seventh day of the week**. No work could be done on this day, or on any other day that God had described as Holy. Instead, they congregated into groups and listened as the Priests taught them from the book of the law. These were times for worship and the family and included feasting and fellowship with solemn observance of "strange rituals". **These rituals contained a much deeper meaning than was generally understood by the average Israelite** and its only in the days that we're living in now that we're able to comprehend the full significance of why God had established them. There was divine purpose behind everything they were instructed to do. They didn't know it yet but God was using ISRAEL to reveal amazing truths to His future people and to the wider nations.

The nation of Israel was formed from 12 families, or tribes, which grew into a nation of millions. Two of these tribes came from the families of Judah and Levi; the Jews and the Levites. The modern state of Israel is largely formed from the modern-day descendants of these two tribes. The modern-day descendants of the other ten tribes are broadly spread among the nations of the West in parts of Europe, the UK and Commonwealth nations and the USA. I know this fact is widely disputed but it's difficult to understand future prophetic events until Bible students have checked this out for themselves.

ANCIENT MEDIA

Whenever Israel got themselves into trouble, God would send Prophets (messengers and fore-tellers of future events) to warn them about their behaviour and urge them to repent and go back to keeping the law. **Included in these messages were visions of future events**. So the prophets were not just warning the EXISTING people about their behaviour and the potential consequences they were storing up for themselves, their messages also contained future visions relevant to OUR time. God was laying out His plan for Mankind in "News Bulletins" given to certain individuals at different times. **These news bulletins were about things that hadn't happened yet**, it's like hearing a news broadcast about tomorrow's events the night before.

The Prophets wrote down what they saw using familiar imagery and descriptions based on the world around them. They may have seen visions about what was going to happen in the future but they couldn't describe them using the terminology we know today, **they could only describe them using terms commonly used in their own culture**. This is one of the reasons why the Bible can sometimes sound so strange.

For instance, if you take a modern-day car back in time, 1,000 years before the birth of Christ, and asked these people to describe this car in their own words, this is probably what they would say: "I saw a breathing monster that blew smoke from its rear and was decorated with gleaming breastplates and armour. It sped swiftly across the desert, never lifting its nose from the earth." He had just described an ordinary family saloon with the shock and wide-eyed wonder of a child. But **he had to use his own language to describe what he had just seen** because he'd never heard of words like cars, automobiles, planes, bombs or anything else that we commonly use today.

It's so important that we take this into account when we're seeking to understand Biblical prophecy and try to visualise what these prophets were actually seeing at the time they saw it.

Much of the prophecy written about in the Old Testament related to a major event that was just around the corner. God the Son was about to come down to Earth and be born to a young, unmarried virgin from the tribe of Judah.

SUMMARY OF PART FIVE

Uninspired human solutions bring unintended consequences.

All modern-day nations are related to Noah and his family . . .

God set a rainbow in the sky as a promise to us and a reminder to Himself, that He would never flood the Whole Earth again.

The main reason behind this explosion of knowledge was the fact that EVERYBODY SPOKE THE SAME LANGUAGE.

The Global Language of NUMBERS has now been harnessed by Computers and the Internet . . . 666 !

The modern-day descendants of Ephraim are the United Kingdom of Great Britain, the Commonwealth and principalities of the UK. The modern-day descendants of Manasseh are the United States of America and her principalities.

THE WILL OF GOD FOR ALL HUMANITY IS TO CHOOSE TO LIVE BY THE LOVE OF GOD CODIFIED INTO THE PRINCIPLES SET FORTH WITHIN THE TEN COMMANDMENTS . . .

The physical act of murder is merely the outward expression of what was already in the heart.

Execution satisfied the law and no further judgement would be brought on that wider society.

These rituals enabled Israel to have a relationship with God and formed the basis of the covenant between God and Israel but it excluded anyone else.

If a nation conveyed gifts and honour to Israel, God would accept this as honour toward Himself and deliberately bless the nation that behaved in this way.

Within these Special Days were laid the foundation of God's redemptive plan for the WHOLE OF MANKIND.

MAN CELEBRATES EVENTS OF THE PAST . . . GOD CELEBRATES EVENTS IN THE FUTURE !!!

They didn't know it yet but God was using ISRAEL to reveal amazing truths to His future people and to the wider nations.

PART SIX

From Death to Life

The King of all Creation was coming, IN HUMAN FORM.

The account of His arrival and what He did in His life can be found in the Gospels (that's Matthew, Mark, Luke and John). We are concerned with WHY He came. He divested Himself of all His power. He was conceived by the Holy Spirit to an unmarried virgin and was born in very poor circumstances. His arrival was heralded (or announced) by Angels to a group of shepherds looking after sheep on a hillside. These were poor people, despised people, illiterate people, yet God chose to announce the greatest event in the Universe to THEM.

From the moment He arrived, Jesus the Christ was identified with those who were looked down upon by the rest of society.

GOD WAS *NOT* WELCOME

Now where was Satan while all this was happening? He was fully aware of these events and his gift for this occasion was both typical and tragic. The Roman Governor of the area where Jesus was born had heard that **a pretender to his throne had been born (sound familiar?),** so fearing the loss of his position, King Herod ordered the murder of every male child aged two and under in Bethlehem and the surrounding districts. Jesus the Christ had arrived, born among the poor and oppressed. His arrival was greeted with fear, suspicion, scepticism and murder.

He then did what the Israelites, or any other man for that matter, couldn't do. He went on to live a perfect, sinless life. He kept the whole law absolutely perfectly, not a single error. He dotted every 'i' and crossed every 't'.

During His three and a half year ministry, that began in His 30th year, He healed the sick, cast out demons and raised the dead. He taught that the greatest enemy that Man has to face is himself.

Before Jesus came along, no one had any idea that there was a being called God-the-Father. Jesus came to reveal the Father and referred to Himself as both **the Son-of-Man (through Mary, His human mother) and the Son-of-God (through His Heavenly Father)**. Remember, Jesus Christ had no earthly father, there was no male sperm involved in his production as a human being.

Jesus taught that the whole of mankind was going to have to be reconciled to the Father and **that would only be possible through Jesus Christ**. Because, no man or woman would ever be able to have access to the Father unless they were completely sinless and totally clean.

The world had lived with the terrible consequences of sin for 4,000 years, up to that time. **For all that to be cleaned up, someone had to pay.** Someone whose life was worth more than the sum total of every man, woman and child that had ever lived and ever will live. The sins of countless generations would be washed clean in blood!

BETTER THAN SUPERMAN

The life that Jesus lived was perfect, without sin, completely unblemished. In terms of the law, He was utterly blameless, totally innocent. Yet, for the sake of Mankind, **He took it upon Himself to be made the scape-goat for everything we had ever done**. The final agonising hours of Jesus Christ are documented as a testimony to the world of the price that had to be paid for our sinful condition which was a debt that we could not possibly pay.

God-the-Father demonstrated His love for humanity by sending His only Son to pay that debt in our stead and thereby saving us from the consequences of sin and the final penalty of eternal death. He went to the cross willingly, for our sake, for humanity's sake. **An act of love without parallel in all human history**.

When Jesus was resurrected back to life after His crucifixion, He spent a little more time with His disciples (students, protege) before ascending back to the Heavenly Realm to be with His Father. A little time later, on the Feast of Pentecost, **His followers miraculously received the gift of the Holy Spirit**. This was effectively the presence of Jesus Christ living within them.

You see, the Holy Spirit IS God's presence.

RIGHTEOUS REAL-ESTATE

Under the Old Covenant, **the Lord (the one who became Jesus Christ) placed His presence into a moment of time**. This moment of time occurred once a week on the Sabbath. The Sabbath was made Holy because the Lord had placed His presence into that 24 hour period. Another example of Holiness is when Moses encountered the burning bush. This was the story where Moses was walking along one day and he found a bush was on fire, nothing unusual in that, except that the fire was not consuming the bush. It was burning away but the bush was completely unhurt and when he went to investigate, God revealed that He was there in the fire and Moses was told to remove his shoes because **he was standing on Holy ground**. But, as soon as the Lord left, the ground was no longer Holy.

Under the New Covenant, which is what Christians live under today, **the presence of God is now placed into His people**. The ones who believe and follow the example and teachings of Jesus Christ. So now, it is the people that have been made Holy because the presence of God resides within them. This does not mean Christians are perfect, it simply means they have been called out, chosen and set aside for a special purpose. It also means Christians have access to the Father through their relationship with Jesus Christ. **His blood covers their sins making them clean**. The Holy Spirit also empowers Christians to get rid of bad habits, wrong actions, wrong thinking and wrong speaking.

They are the NEW priesthood of believers, empowered and authorised to intercede on behalf of the afflicted of this world and on behalf of each other. **The Church is God's gift to mankind**, which is why you will see Christian organisations working in some of the most hostile and miserable places on Earth because we see it as our duty and responsibility to look out for the welfare of hurting people all over the world and alleviate suffering wherever we can.

We're also granted super-natural assistance to aid those we are seeking to help.

NO RITUAL RESURRECTION

The Old Covenant, or contractual agreement, between Israel and God was based on physical blessings for obedience and physical suffering for disobedience. The whole nation was still under the Law, just as all the other nations of the world are. **What was unique about Israel was that they KNEW about this Law**, where-as no other nation was really aware of it, even though these Laws were planet-wide. Israel was the nation chosen by God to abide by and implement the sacrificial system that was uniquely designed to foreshadow everything that Jesus Christ did throughout His life and through the manner of His death. But, **when He died, the Old Covenant as it was called, this agreement, the Old Covenant died with Him!** So the Old Covenant is no longer in existence.

Under the New Covenant, Christians do not have to slaughter animals to atone for their sins. Instead, the perfect blood of Jesus Christ covers their sins upon confession and repentance. **Religious symbols have been replaced by Faith**. Circumcision and the Sabbath Day, as the defining characteristics of being the people of God, has been replaced by unity and love (Agapé).

Do the laws still exist that govern human behaviour? Absolutely. **The nations of this world are still under the Law and they're still punished or rewarded according to their behaviour under these laws whether they know about them or not**, otherwise there would be no sin and nothing to repent of. The people of the Church (Christians) however, live under Grace, a state of undeserved forgiveness. But they also have responsibilities that the rest of the world doesn't have. Those responsibilities will be spelled out in a later chapter.

Most of the New Testament part of the Bible is concerned with the activities of the early Christian Church, their experiences and teachings. The word "Church", by the way, comes from the Greek word *"ecclesiaste"* which simply means "the group of called-out ones". It is not supposed to refer to a building, although many structures have been built that are called churches because men and women of God would congregate there for regular meetings.

It should be noted that these "church" buildings, however elaborate their architecture, do not possess any special qualities, in spite of what you may have seen in Hollywood movies. They are not "Holy places". God does not RESIDE within these buildings. **He has placed His Spirit within people NOT in bricks and mortar**.

SATAN IS AT WAR WITH THE CHURCH

Two thousand years have passed since the events took place as described in the New Testament. Christianity has become an accepted religion by most parts of the world, but its history has been bloody and filled with violence and many things have been done in the name of Christ that would shock most unbelievers.

There seems to be very little unity among Christian groups and even less when it comes to specific teachings, known as doctrines. So, why is there so much division and confusion? **Because the enemy of both God and Man fears a unified church and he has worked to corrupt and intimidate its followers.**

Nowhere is this better illustrated than in the traditional Christian teaching on what happens after death.

HELLISH STATISTICS

Since the time of Adam and Eve to the present day, approximately 40 billion people have lived and died. **One of the basic teachings of modern-day, traditional Christianity (taught over many generations) has been the concept of Heaven and Hell**. Under this teaching, those who have accepted Jesus Christ as their personal Saviour will go to Heaven when they die. Apparently, they will live on some ethereal plane, probably playing harps and not doing very much. For those who have not made that choice, their fate, upon death, is to be sent to some fiery hole located somewhere near the centre of the Earth where

Satan and his demons are supposed to live. There, they will live forever in perpetual torment, lost forever. Now that's the traditional teaching and it's been taught that way for at least the last 1,500 years. Its a flat-earth theory that has persisted right up until our present day and it's time for it to be abandoned and replaced with Biblical truth.

You see, whoever conceived of such a teaching did so without examining certain facts.

Remember I told you that the Bible is written like a huge jigsaw puzzle. If you don't get the overall picture, you will fall into error and start believing ridiculous scenarios like the Heaven and Hell concept.

This concept ignores the fact that **for every Spirit-born Christian that has ever lived, since Adam and Eve, there have been TEN THOUSAND non-Christians**. It ignores the fact that, prior to the sacrifice of Jesus Christ, nearly 5 billion people had lived and died without ever having heard of the New Covenant, let alone being able to participate in it.

Over the last 2,000 years, in spite of the best efforts of zealous missionaries, **billions of people have lived and died without ever having heard the name of Jesus Christ**, much less listened to, understood and fully comprehended the original gospel (the Christian message of Jesus Christ). Even in the Western world, there has been a huge disparity between those that have heard the gospel and those that have actually understood it. And, of those that HAVE understood it, only a tiny minority have ever actually responded to the point where they have made Jesus the Lord of their lives and followed His ways.

If the Heaven and Hell concept is to be believed, **this would mean that 95% of the entire human population that has ever lived has been consigned to an eternal life of torment and misery**. Can you believe that? If true, what does this say about our Creator? That He delights in human suffering? That He rejoices at losing 95% of His human family to His Arch-enemy Satan?

What about Jesus Christ? His life could not have been worth as much as the Bible has led us to believe if His sacrifice only applies to 5% of the world's population. It would also mean that the Arch-angel Gabriel lied to the shepherds on the hilltop. It also means that most of the prophecies in the Bible (making up nearly one-third of the whole Bible) are a pack of lies and therefore NONE of the Bible can be trusted. **Who do you think is responsible for this kind of warped thinking?** Who enjoys making God look bad? Who lied to one-third of all the Angels and set them against their Creator? Who lied to Eve in the Garden of Eden and set us upon this destructive course in the first place?

Satan!

Satan is the arch-enemy of Man.

Sometimes, his lies and deceits have got the better of Christian men who should have known better.

The traditional concept of Heaven and Hell is utterly False! The truth is very different and it portrays our Heavenly Father and our Saviour in Their TRUE LIGHT.

DEATH IN TRANSITION

To understand what really happens when someone dies, we have to skip forward to a time in the not-too-distant future when, as prophesied, Jesus Christ returns to this Earth.

Just prior to His return, Mankind will have brought himself to the brink of almost total destruction. Wars will have been fought with even greater destructive power than has ever been seen before. There will have been a huge proliferation of biological weapons creating wide-spread disease, famine and consequent economic and social disaster.

There will have been a complete loss of self-restraint, allowing every form of evil and wicked thought to be acted out. This will be a time of anarchy, which we have seen before in smaller conflicts, the only difference this time is that it will be on a global scale.

To show just how far from God humanity has gone, the Bible reveals that a huge army will be assembled to fight Jesus Christ when He returns. Our Saviour, the One who died for us, is not going to receive a very warm welcome when He comes back. But this time, **He does not come as a little child but as King of kings and Lord of lords** and everyone will be able to see Him when He returns. Also, He does not come alone. He returns with tens of thousands of His Saints. Every Spirit-born Christian, disciple and prophet that had served God faithfully during their lives will have been resurrected into their eternal inheritance.

A "RAPTUROUS" RECEPTION

That FIRST resurrection would also have removed living worthy Christians from off the Earth just before the final judgement on this present age starts. **They will be with Jesus and their bodies will be comprised of spirit**, no longer subject to aging or death or confined by the laws of matter.

Once the uprising has been put down, the remnant of people still alive on the Earth will be in a pretty sorry state: injured, bewildered, sick and terrified. **But they now find themselves at the mercy of a New-World Order that is built on love, compassion, mercy, justice**

and righteousness. They will be looked after and they will start to participate in the re-building of a shattered world under the guidance and benevolent leadership of Jesus Christ and His Saints. They will initiate, direct and supervise the building of new communities, farms and cities.

SATAN IN TARTARUS

Around this same time, Satan will be captured and imprisoned, with all the demons, **in a place of restraint** where he will no longer be allowed to influence or oppress Mankind for at least the next 1,000 years. This time, in Biblical terms, is referred to as **the New Millennium**.

With Satan out of the way, families begin to be established. Children are born into the new Eden which is being created around them. There will be no more need for Armies, Police or great burgeoning bureaucracies. There will be no more wars, no more famine. **Disease, illness and disabilities will become a thing of the past as the people learn the RIGHT way to keeping good health**. Each family will have their OWN home and their OWN land. People will have jobs that cater to their skills and interests. Work will be enjoyable and highly rewarding. Business will be conducted where the welfare of the individual supercedes the profit motive. Any potential criminal act will be confronted BEFORE it ever happens and, as families and nations grow, peace and prosperity will reign over the entire Earth.

THE RETURN OF EDEN

The Holy Spirit will be available to everyone so that as they repent and change their lives and grow in the knowledge of God, when their physical lives come to an end, **they will rejoice at the prospect of Eternal Life waiting for them** on the other side.

This will truly be Utopia but everyone will be working and assisting toward the NEXT GREAT STEP in God's plan. **THIS IS THE PART OF THE GOSPEL, THE GOOD NEWS OF THE BIBLE, THAT RARELY EVER GETS MENTIONED** AND YET IT'S CRITICAL TO UNDERSTANDING HOW THE PLAN OF REDEMPTION WILL ACTUALLY WORK.

Under Jesus, the Saints will not only be administering rule over the people, teaching and helping them fulfill their potential, they will also be involved in huge construction works to supply accommodation, food, clothing and equipment to provide for the initial needs of A GIGANTIC SUDDEN INFLUX OF BILLIONS UPON BILLIONS OF PEOPLE.

To ensure adequate space, mountains will be lowered, oceans will be reduced in size and all the desert places will be turned into parklands where every green thing will flourish. At the present time, nearly two-thirds of the surface of the Earth is completely uninhabited. By the time this preparation work is finished, that would apply to only 15% of the total surface of the Earth.

From the time of the return of Jesus Christ to completion of this preparation, will be about 900 years. THE WORLD IS NOW READY . . .

YES, FUNERAL *WAS* AN ANAGRAM

Now let's skip back to a very ordinary event in our recent history to demonstrate **what ACTUALLY happens when someone dies:**

"The year is 1915. The world has been at war for almost 12 months. A young French soldier has spent 6 miserable months living in a sea of mud, climbing over the top of his trench to attack the enemy and recoiling at the brutal sight of slain comrades scattered around the field of battle. He is sick with dysentery, yet his commanding officer tells him he must attack. He misses the beautiful girl he was going to marry before this wretched war started. His mum and dad need him at the small bakery they run. He longs for the sweet smell of fresh-mown grass and wrestling with his dog Sammy. He wants to hear the birds sing, not bombs exploding. When will it be over?

As he scrambles over the top of his trench, he runs two steps when what feels like a giant hand suddenly slaps him on his left side, throwing him to the ground. He is dazed, confused. He has been shot . . . the wound is fatal. As his life ebbs away, he looks at all the destruction he's leaving behind and he weeps as he imagines how his fiancée will react to the news of his death. The pain is receding, he feels cold, heavy and oh so tired. Everything is blurry, the battle noises sound so distant. His eyes close and he slips into unconsciousness and from there into death"

. . ..The sun feels warm as he wakes up. How long has he been asleep? His side has stopped hurting and there is no sign of the other soldiers. He is lying in a grassy meadow. What is this place? He looks up to see a man sitting just a few feet away. He is smiling, "Welcome," he says, "Let's go and find your family."

The cynic says, "Make the most of this life, you won't get another one". The Word of God says, "It is given to Man once to die and after that will come the judgement".

A SECOND PHYSICAL LIFE?

Everyone, who has ever lived and died, from Adam and Eve to the last one to die at the time of Christ's return will be resurrected back to physical life. Those who have done good AND those who have done great evil.

This period of time, at the end of 900 years, is called: THE LAST

GREAT DAY or THE GREAT WHITE THRONE JUDGEMENT.

From the time of someone's death to the time of this great resurrection, there is no awareness of passing time. **The transition feels instantaneous.** God built this experience into His creation AND ALL HUMAN BEINGS know what it feels like. Anyone, who has gone to bed feeling really tired and closed their eyes and awoke ten hours later, knows what this feels like. YOU HAVE NO CONCEPT OF PASSING TIME.

Death is a very deep sleep, a state of unconsciousness where you could sleep for a thousand years but it passes in less than a second from your last conscious thought (the one prior to death) to your next conscious thought (the one just prior to your waking to the next life).

God could easily have created Man so that he did not need sleep, but **this need for sleep was factored into the physical body so that Man would live with a daily witness to death and resurrection; to sleep and to wake**.

Not for nothing did God say that eternity is written into the heart of Man. We can't comprehend death because it is alien to our spirit. **Even the seasons of the Earth were designed to reflect this part of God's plan.** Nature sleeps in the Winter and arises in the Spring. God also placed this in animals to hibernate during the months of Winter and be "resurrected" back to fulness of life in the Spring. And let's not forget that the planet Earth goes through a 24 hour cycle of day and night that is specifically designed to illustrate the concept of daily death and resurrection. Something that remains until this testing time of human life is over. **Then, and only then, does God change the creation to permanent day-time.**

SUMMARY OF PART SIX

Jesus came to help the poor, the sick and the hurting.

Jesus is the only way by which mankind can be reconciled to God . . .

The church is a group of empowered intercessors whose main purpose in life is to help liberate people from their suffering. Either by miracles or by more conventional means . . .

God has placed His Spirit within people NOT in bricks and mortar.

The enemy of both God and Man fears a unified church and he has worked to corrupt and intimidate its followers.

The Bible is written like a huge jigsaw puzzle. Without the overall picture, we fall into error and destructive heresy . . .

If the Heaven and Hell concept is to be believed, this would mean that 95% of the ENTIRE HUMAN POPULATION, that has ever lived, has been consigned to an eternal life of torment and misery.

The traditional concept of Heaven and Hell is utterly False!

The truth is very different and it portrays our Heavenly Father and our Saviour in Their TRUE LIGHT.

The coming APOCALYPSE will be on a GLOBAL SCALE . . .

This FIRST resurrection only relates to WORTHY Christians, occurring just before the Apocalypse, and is known as "THE RAPTURE".

Satan will be captured and imprisoned, with all the demons, in a place of restraint where he will no longer be allowed to influence or oppress Mankind for at least the next 1,000 years.

The Holy Spirit will be available to EVERYONE, so that as they repent and change their lives and grow in the knowledge of God, when their physical lives come to an end, they will rejoice at the prospect of Eternal Life waiting for them on the other side.

They will also be involved in huge construction works to supply accommodation, food, clothing and equipment to provide for the initial needs of A GIGANTIC SUDDEN INFLUX OF BILLIONS UPON BILLIONS OF PEOPLE.

From the time of the return of Jesus Christ to completion of this preparation, it will be about 900 years. THE WORLD IS NOW READY . . .

The cynic says, "Make the most of this life, you won't get another one".

The Word of God says, "It is given to Man once to die and after that will come the judgement".

This period of time, at the end of 900 years, is called: THE LAST GREAT DAY or THE GREAT WHITE THRONE JUDGEMENT.

Death is a very deep state of unconsciousness where you could sleep for a thousand years but it passes in less than a second.

This need for sleep was factored into the physical body so that Man would live with a daily witness to death and RESURRECTION; to sleep and to WAKE.

PART SEVEN

Revealing the Children of God

So every human being that has ever lived, but was not raised in the FIRST resurrection, will be brought back to life. From Adam and Eve right up to the last human being, ALL WILL BE MADE ALIVE.

The purpose of this SECOND physical life is JUDGEMENT, NOT CONDEMNATION, Judgement. **The Bible refers to this 100 year period as the LAST GREAT DAY or THE GREAT WHITE THRONE JUDGEMENT**. Up to 50 billion people will be living on this Earth ALL AT ONCE, all at the same time. Whether someone died as a baby or an old man, ALL will live for one hundred years in this second life . . .

JUDGEMENT – EXPERIENCE, TEST, CONCLUSION

And this is what everyone will be told:

> *"You have spent your first life doing as you pleased. You have lived under a curse because you have been separated from your God. You have hurt yourselves and each other. All creation has suffered because of your ignorant and rebellious ways. Now, in this second life, you will live for 100 years, regardless of whether you are a child or an old man, you will all live for the same period of time.*

You will not bear children for the fulness of procreation has now been accomplished. Instead, you will learn to live according to the Word of God and you will be judged throughout this Second life according to what is written in the Word of God.

Every evil act from your first life will be exposed, every harm you have ever done will be made known. Things done in secret places will be brought out into the open. Each shall have this opportunity to do good and see for himself that God's way is the best way.

During this period everyone, without exception, will have the opportunity to receive Jesus Christ as their personal Saviour, to have their sins forgiven and to receive the Holy Spirit. In this new life, there is no deception. The only things being taught is that which is true and honourable. Your Saviour Jesus Christ is responsible for this amazing opportunity to contrast this SECOND life lived under His benevolent, righteous government and the tragic circumstances of your FIRST life. Learn the lesson well and embrace His amazing grace."

ONLY FOR A LITTLE SEASON

Toward the end of this 100 year period of this SECOND life, **in order to complete the testing of Man**, God will release Satan back into the Earth.

Astonishing as it may seem, **there will still be people who will prefer what Satan offers them** rather than submit to God's rule over their lives. This last final test is what is used to bring out these people's true heart. These are the incorrigible. If God were to allow them to live beyond this life, **they would wreak havoc in His creation** and cause great harm to His family.

So, at the end of this period of testing, the entire Earth is consumed by fire. **Everyone is still on Earth when this fire breaks out**. Fire rains down from the skies and explodes out of the centre of the Earth but it only has power to consume the incorrigible. **The fire does not**

have power over anyone else because they have passed the final test and their existence has suddenly passed from the physical into the Spiritual plane.

The Bible refers to this all-consuming fire as **Gehenna or hellfire** and it consumes everything, including Satan and his demons. They do not go into some torture chamber, they are simply extinguished as if they had never existed.

God is merciful, even to the very end.

FROM PAIN TO ETERNAL PARADISE

So, the Plan of God is complete and Eternal Life can now begin in earnest. People sometimes speculate about eternity **wondering what they could possibly find to do with all that time**. Well, remember that God has created the Universe which is so vast that its size is completely beyond our comprehension. There are billions upon billions of planets, all of them different, all of them needing the powerful creative touch of the Children of God.

Then, there are relationships. Every one of us will have a story to tell. Suppose you decided to get to know one new person every day. You could start, on the first day, by visiting the Planet Saturn and then stop for dinner on Mars while you reminisce about each other's lives. The next day, you do something similar with someone else. So that means it would take you 50 billion days or 137 million years to spend just one day with everyone in your family and, when you had finished, it would be time to start all over again. This is not fantasy, this is the Word of God and this tiny description barely scrapes the surface of what our Heavenly Father has in store for His Children.

I started out by telling you that God wants a family. His Will will be accomplished. Jesus Christ is central to everything. Nothing, no one, will slip through the cracks. God has thought of everything. Throughout the remainder of this book we will be going into much greater detail on some of the questions that this summary raises.

WHEN TRUTH SETS US FREE

But, before we get to that, let's review the 12 questions that we started with and see if we're any closer to the answers:

1) *Why did God create me?*
A) **He wants a family and He's looking at you and me as His potential Son/Daughter.**

2) *If God exists, why does He allow so much suffering?*
A) **He has given Man free moral agency. We have the right to make choices in our life, whether for good or for evil. If we defer to God's instructions and live by His decree, we, and our loved ones, can have a pretty good life. If we rely on our own wisdom, we're led astray and the consequences are awful.**

3) *You say there is one God, then how come there are so many religions?*
A) **There is Satanic deception throughout the world. All human beings are created with a God-shaped hole in their lives and they need to fill it with something. So, until they have a personal encounter with God through Jesus Christ, they will gravitate toward anything that promises to fill it. Look closely at any other religion and you very quickly find just how MAN-MADE it really is.**

4) *I live in a nation where half the people are starving, the crops have failed and civil war is rampant. How will knowing God's plan change this situation?*
A) **Right knowledge is key. One man can change around an entire nation just by building a vision for the future that inspires the people to action. We know that dark spiritual forces are behind much of the evil**

on this Earth, the Church has been empowered to counter that. One righteous man submitted to God and led by His Holy Spirit can pray effectively for his nation and begin to turn it around.

5) *My son was a multiple murderer and committed suicide. Will I ever see him again?*

A) Yes, you will, in the Great White Throne Judgement. This is the 100 year period I spoke of earlier. Then he will be given the opportunity for repentance and to learn a new and better way of living.

6) *I cannot stand injustice, but I know men that have raped, tortured, stolen, cheated and lied and yet they are prospering. Can God explain this?*

A) No one gets away with anything (see our book: *Exposing the Curse*). But evil often prospers well beyond its sell-by date because, instead of turning to God to be their vindicator, the victims and their families pursue their own remedies and help propagate evil by ignoring the ways of God and refusing to turn to Him for repentance and justice.

7) *My friend never received Jesus Christ as her personal saviour, but she spent her life helping others. She has since died, has she gone to hell?*

A) No. She will have her opportunity for personal salvation during the Great White Throne Judgement. The current teaching on Hell is a discredited doctrine that even the Bible doesn't support. The scriptural analysis for this assertion will begin to be dealt with in the next chapter.

8) *Eternal Life may sound good, but what will we spend eternity doing?*

A) We have already looked briefly at this with regard to our relationships with one another. There is the exploration of the entire Universe. All the planets are un-finished and lifeless, we will be changing that. There's the enhancement of knowledge and growing in skills and talents and that's without mentioning a vast Spiritual realm that none of us have ever seen or could even imagine. It will be an awesome experience and it's going to last forever. Who would want to miss out on that?

9) *When we take the sum total of every man, woman and child that has ever lived, or is living now, we find that less than one in every 200 people, across the world are, or have been, committed Christians. Isn't the devil winning hands-down with less than 1% of the total world population making it into heaven?*

A) Exactly. The current doctrine just doesn't stand up to scrutiny which is why we have had to do this presentation. The fact is; God is only working with a comparatively small number of people at this time. He isn't trying to get everyone converted. He chooses the people HE wants and prepares them for service now and in the future. Remember the Bride and the marriage come first, THEN you have the children. As in Christ's ministry, many people will receive a powerful witness through miraculous healing or deliverance from a difficult situation but that won't necessarily translate into total conversion.

10) *My sister was sexually abused as a child, put on the street as a prostitute at the age of 12 and is now dying of AIDS and other STDs. How can God help her?*

A) Powerful, intercessory prayer by a group of Bible-believing, faith-filled Christians on her behalf. I know it works, I've done it. More information can be found in our book: *Miraculous Healing for the Church*.

11) *The animals, the birds & the fish in the sea haven't done anything wrong, so why do they suffer and do they go to heaven when they die?*

A) Mankind was given dominion over all the animals, birds and sea-life. Everything we do affects them. Their suffering is a testimony against us. Jesus has promised to restore everything that has been lost or destroyed as a consequence of our sin. Nothing is impossible with God and I think that our Creator, who is also THEIR Creator, has made provision for them to experience an Eden-like existence as well

as the whole of Mankind, before or during the Great White Throne Judgement period.

12) *Disability, illness and disease are a fact of life for millions of people, even today, what can God do for them?*

A) **Turn back to God. Confess your sins and start to change your ways. Solicit help from your local church. Listen and act upon their advice so long as it originates from the Bible. Forgive those who have offended you and look for opportunities to serve others who are in trouble. This repentant attitude and action will spark a series of events that will lead to your deliverance if you relentlessly pursue it.**

The Bible is a sound source of inspiration and advice for any individual, family, community and nation on Earth. It is trust-worthy and reliable and reflects the nature and character of our Creator.

Don't allow inaccurate interpretations and uninspired teaching to cause you to mis-trust the Bible. Man is fallible, God is Not!!!!

So let's do a very brief re-cap of the whole story:

This summary has been built around the fact that God hasn't just revealed himself and his plans through the bible but also through his physical creation. One of the references to this can be found in Romans 1:20:

"For since the creation of the world, His invisible attributes are clearly seen, being understood by the things that are made, even His eternal power and Godhead so that they are without excuse."

But the Bible itself must be the defining authority of the Christian faith, its a very practical book that is frighteningly accurate about EVERY subject that it covers. Its warnings, claims and advice should always be taken seriously.

To DISTINGUISH TRUTH FROM ERROR we should let the bible interpret the bible. When we do that, we uncover Gods plans which are hidden in a mosaic of gems spread throughout His word, very much like a great big Jigsaw Puzzle which has to be put together in the right order. This presentation was designed to show you what the finished picture is supposed to look like.

IT starts with the fact that God wants a family of BILLIONS of children.

His children will be spirits, endowed with creative ability and motivated by Godly love. But they must also be able to exercise freedom of choice. So His children must freely choose to adopt God's perfect ways as their own ways, so that the family of God is One in total unity.

The only way to create that was to give His children a very brief taste of life as physical beings where they could make their choices and experience the consequences.

SO, CREATION BEGAN WITH THE ANGELS.

To ably assist God, the angels would also need to exercise free-will.

Now their test was whether they would cooperate with God and work with Him to accomplish His purpose of creating His family, or would they rebel?

An archangel called Lucifer was given dominion over the Earth, but He resented God's plan. So he turned ALL the angels on Earth against God and led them in an attempt to over-throw God Himself.

The Earth and the Cosmos was devastated by this rebellion. But God restored the Earth and prepared it for human habitation.

Then God created the very first man and woman called Adam and Eve and placed them in a beautiful location called Eden which literally means Paradise.

The entire human race can be traced back to Adam. Every human child born to woman has the potential to become an eternal child of God.

Lucifer became Satan who lied to Eve and got her to influence her husband to sin. As a consequence they were cast out of paradise and now had to fend for themselves.

Mankind has been separated from God ever since and our conduct has been governed by eternal, spiritual laws that bring curses for disobedience and blessings for compliance with these laws whether we're aware of them or not.

Death was permanent and held no prospect of future life. But God had a plan of redemption, not just for Adam and Eve but for the whole of humanity.

God's answer for the hopelessness of the human condition was to send Jesus Christ who was literally God in the flesh. He lived His life without sin and was then executed, putting Himself in our place.

Just as the whole of humanity was condemned through the sin of Adam, the whole of humanity would now be saved through Jesus Christ.

The choice for people now is whether or not to believe that Jesus has paid the debt for their sins. If they choose to believe and trust God, confess their sins and start turning their lives around, God will heal our bodies, our minds, our relationships and cause us to prosper.

Jesus is the only way by which mankind can be reconciled to God . . .

The job of the church is to help liberate people from their suffering. Either by miracles, testimonies and teachings from the Bible or by more conventional means . . .

Our present lives can be made much happier if we accept and believe this good news. For those who don't or can't accept it. They will get their chance during their second physical life in The Great White Throne Judgement, when everyone who wasn't chosen in this life will be resurrected.

The testing of humanity is concluded at the end of this period and those who still stubbornly refuse God's rulership over their lives will be lost forever.

For everyone else, Eternal Life will begin and God will have the family of billions of God children that He always wanted.

Now, before we conclude this summary, I want to look very briefly at **Revelation, chapter 13, verse 18** which refers to the number of the Beast 666. There has been a huge amount of conjecture over what this refers to, but I personally think that Jesus (who gave the revelation to John) has had a quiet chuckle over some of the outlandish theories that have been proposed, because the answer is so obvious it's almost laughable.

You see, 666 is the number of a man . . . get it?

666 is the number . . . of a man, **of any man**, of all men who are not set apart by the Holy Spirit. Simple really. And what do the 3 sixes refer to?

Man was created on the 6th day. Man will labour for 6 days and do all his work, and finally, Man is allotted 6,000 years to live his own way before God takes over.

In verse 16, we're told that a mark is placed on the right-hand and on the forehead of all those who worship the Beast. The right-hand signifies the work of Man, the forehead signifies Man's reasoning, or his thoughts.

You see, in the Bible, six signifies Man as a completed PHYSICAL being. But God doesn't want a number six man, He wants a glorified, spiritually complete, child-of God Man, which is signified by the number seven.

Just something for you Bible students to chew on.

SUMMARY OF PART SEVEN

This period of time is known as the Millennium, or 1,000 years where the entire Earth will be transformed into a veritable Garden of Eden.

The purpose of this SECOND physical life is JUDGEMENT, NOT CONDEMNATION.

The Bible refers to this 100 year period as the LAST GREAT DAY or THE GREAT WHITE THRONE JUDGEMENT.

Up to 50 billion people will be living on this Earth ALL AT ONCE, all at the same time.

Toward the end of this 100 year period of this SECOND life, IN ORDER TO COMPLETE THE TESTING OF MAN, God will release Satan back into the Earth.

The Bible refers to this all-consuming fire as Gehenna or hellfire and it consumes everything, including Satan and his demons. They do not go into some torture chamber, they are simply extinguished as if they had never existed.

THE TESTING IS OVER and ETERNAL LIFE can begin in earnest.

Don't allow inaccurate interpretations and uninspired teaching to cause you to mis-trust the Bible. Man is fallible, God is Not!!!!

"God hasn't just revealed himself and his plans through the bible but also through his physical creation."

But His children must freely choose to adopt God's perfect ways as their own ways.

Death was permanent and held no prospect of future life.

But God had a plan of redemption, not just for Adam and Eve but for the whole of humanity.

God will have the family of billions of God children that He always wanted.

God doesn't want a number 6 man, He wants a glorified, spiritually complete, child-of God Man, which is signified by the number 7.

Digesting the Answers

It would be fair to say that many of my readers will be incredulous at what they have read up to now, because it seems to be such a departure from what they have learned in the past.

But none of this is idle speculation and, believe it or not, none of this is new. This was known by Jesus, the Apostles and most of the members of the Early church. This book is not about NEW knowledge, this is about RECOVERED knowledge and it has enormous implications for how the gospel (Good News) is to be preached from this point on.

Where to From Here?

We've looked at a brief synopsis of the entire Bible story. The next part deals with all the questions thrown up about justice and vengeance.

These questions will inevitably be raised because much of the theoretical justification for the traditional teaching on hell is based on punishment of the wicked.

Finally, we will review every single scripture that has ever been used to prop up this traditional teaching and check context and application. The conclusions are truly astonishing. And finally, we re-state the gospel (Good News) as it will need to be taught from this point on, using scripture only . . .

PART EIGHT

"Eternal Deceits"

THE DOCTRINE OF VENGEANCE

When someone carries out a truly wicked and evil act, especially against someone smaller and weaker, we comfort ourselves with the thought that God will bring him into eternal torment and misery (Hell) when he passes from this life to the next.

We will heap curses and insults onto his head, praying for his death and salivating at the thought of all those tortures that will one day be inflicted upon him for ever and ever.

Traditional religious teaching encourages this view, including much of Christianity. Unfortunately, for all who believe this way, the foundation for these feelings is a very understandable desire for vengeance. But it isn't divine vengeance, it's a very powerful human desire, drawn from the deepest recesses of human nature.

As we've already seen from the preceding summary of the Bible story, this idea of an eternity of torture (Hell) just doesn't stack up. All repercussions for evil performed in this life, **are punished in THIS life**. If not on the perpetrator directly, then on his progeny, his loved ones. This may not be how we would deal with it but God has set a divine justice system in motion that no one can escape. So let's see if we can prove this through Real-Life experiences and scriptural analysis . . .

Now God clearly says, "Vengeance is MINE, I will repay those who have practised iniquity." Isn't this statement a tick in the yes column for eternal damnation? Many traditionalists believe that it is. Shortly, we will be looking at all the scriptures that are used to justify this position, how they came to these conclusions and why the Bible itself does NOT support these conclusions. But first, we need to see **the HUMAN reasoning that contributed to the traditionalist view** that has held sway for over 1,500 years:

Religious scholars have debated and argued the following points for centuries. In the brief summary below, I have highlighted the points that these scholars do agree on. From a Christian perspective, these points have been broadly accepted and taught to the wider Christian church. The reader should note that these points, at this stage of the book, are philosophical and NOT scriptural. We will deal with the scriptural analysis later on in this book:

The following quotes are based on writings sourced from: "On the belief of all nations in the existence of hell" cf. Lüken, *Die Traditionen des Menschengeschlechts* (2nd ed., Münster, 1869); Knabenbauer, *Das Zeugnis des Menschengeschlechts fur die Unsterblichkeit der Seele* (1878)

THE JUSTICE ARGUMENT

They have stated that:

> . . .*if we use human reasoning as the basis for eternal punishment, we can easily justify the existence of hell. After all, if God is to avenge the violation of the moral order in such a way as to preserve, at least in general, some proportion between the gravity of sin and the severity of punishment, it is evident from experience that God does not always do this on Earth; therefore He will inflict punishment after death. We can all point to examples where*

someone appears to have escaped punishment by dying before he had received his full due for all the crimes he had committed."

This argument is spurious and uninformed and is thoroughly rebutted by scripture in my book: *Exposing the Curse.*

THE ANARCHY ARGUMENT

They also state that:

. . .we also have to consider that if all men are fully convinced that the sinner need fear no kind of punishment after death, moral and social order could be seriously undermined. The threat of eternal damnation is a useful tool for social order.

Also, if there were no retribution beyond what we witness here on Earth, we would have to consider that God is extremely indifferent to good and evil and we could, in no way, account for His justice and holiness.

It is further argued that positive punishment is the natural recompense of evil. In other words, death is not enough. If the just are to be rewarded beyond this life, then it stands to reason that the unjust will be punished beyond this life.

Again, most of these points are rebutted in the book I've just mentioned. As to the point that the just will be rewarded beyond this life . . . This only applies to Christians who have faithfully followed the teachings of Jesus Christ and been faithful in their part of the Great Commission. **However, if Christians disregard instruction and fail in their "reasonable service" and end up completely turning their back on Christ, they DO expose themselves to a judgement that will have Eternal consequences.**

But this situation does not apply to unbelievers who remain under the Law.

John 12v47: And if anyone hears My words and does not believe, I DO NOT JUDGE HIM; for I did not come to judge the World but to save the World.

v48: He who rejects Me, and does not receive My words, has that which judges him (THE CONSEQUENCES OF THE LAW) the word that I have spoken will judge him in THE LAST DAY. (Reference to the LAST GREAT DAY RESURRECTION).

Any argument to the contrary is making God out to be a liar and His Word untrustworthy. A very clear case of whether we choose to believe God or Man.

THE PROPORTIONALITY ARGUMENT

They insist that:

> there has to be due proportion between the gravity of the sin and the punishment that follows. However, this proportionality would be rendered impossible by indiscriminate annihilation of all the wicked. So the argument goes that hell will be eternal torment that will exact from the offender the due proportion of his offence.

> Finally, if men knew that their sins would not be followed by sufferings, the mere threat of annihilation at the moment of death, and still less the prospect of a somewhat lower degree of reward, would be insufficient to deter them from sin."

Regrettably, I'm forced to agree about the deterrent theme as being insufficient to persuade some people away from sin. Parents know what that is like. You can warn a teenager 'til you're blue in the face about the consequences of drugs or pre-marital sex, but they'll go out and do it anyway.

Without the super-natural assistance of the Holy Spirit giving us

both the desire and the means to follow the ways of God, warnings by themselves will never be enough. That's why many people won't even consider repentance until they've begun to experience the consequences of their wrong choices.

But threatening eternal consequences, especially when it isn't true, won't have much of an effect either.

As far as the "proportionality" arguments go, these DO take place in THIS life and are documented in my book: *Exposing the Curse*.

THE "EVERYBODY CAN'T BE WRONG" ARGUMENT

They further go on to state that:

> *Accordingly, we find among all nations and religions the belief that evil-doers will be punished after death. This universal conviction of mankind is regarded as an additional proof for the existence of hell. For it is impossible that, in regard to the fundamental questions of their being and their destiny, all men should fall into the same error; else the power of human reason would be essentially deficient, and the order of this world would be unduly wrapt in mystery; this however, is repugnant both to nature and to the wisdom of the Creator."*

Many scriptures in the Bible clearly refute this argument. Satan has deceived the WHOLE WORLD, not just a small part of it. **If we ever get a situation where the whole world, in its present fallen state, agrees on an issue; you can bet your bottom dollar that it's an outright Satanic deception.** For any part of the Christian Church to use the "Everybody-can't-be-wrong" argument to justify anything is unwise. The only way to support such a proposal is to rip the Bible to pieces and burn it.

THE "APOSTASY-OF-DENIERS" ARGUMENT

Finally, they conclude that:

> *The few men who, despite the morally universal conviction of the human race, deny the existence of hell, are mostly atheists and Epicureans. But if the view of such men in the fundamental question of our being could be the true one, apostasy would be the way to light, truth and wisdom."*

The Apostasy-of-deniers argument refuses to accept any other point of view. There is an unwillingness to even consider the possibility that their conclusions may be inaccurate.

Yet knowledge is always evolving and improving as insight and new discoveries better inform us on a whole variety of issues.

This subject is no exception. **The revision of doctrine in the light of new insights and improved understanding is NOT Apostasy.** This attitude of: "Anyone-who-doesn't-agree-with-us-is-a-rebellious-anarchist-who-needs-to-be-burned-at-the-stake" is the kind of thinking that led to the infamous inquisitions of earlier times.

How unfortunate that anyone who believes the Bible over religious dogma is now classified as a heretic.

EXPLANATORY NOTES

Atheism is a wilful rejection of any explanation for a divine entity, as opposed to:

An agnostic who is unconvinced.

Epicurean philosophy is based on observable physical and mental experiences that can be explained without divine input.

My apologies to my readers if you found these arguments difficult to comprehend (you should have seen the originals). I greatly simplified the original explanations to appeal to the broad cross-section of people who will read this book. These arguments are philosophical in nature and were crafted by a scholarly elite who were doubtless seeking to impress one another. You can read the full scriptural rebuttal of these arguments a little further on, **but first, we must address this critical issue of justice and vengeance**.

The simplest way to do that is for me to recount a true story that happened fairly recently. It received worldwide attention and it has plot twists that would fascinate any reader of fiction. I have selected this story because it so beautifully and inadvertently illustrates the conundrum that surround the current teaching on hell . . .

Is This Justice?
The Central-Park Rapist Story

It was April 19th, 1989. On a warm Spring evening Trisha Meili, a 28 year old investment banker, was jogging home from her job at Saloman Brothers, through Central Park in New York. Unbeknown to her, she had caught the eye of a young Latino man, a dangerous sexual predator by the name of Matias Reyes.

He lay in wait for her and then pounced. What followed was an orgy of such frenzied violence that, even today, investigators still find it hard to believe that this was the action of just one man. A 5-foot tall, slim, petite blonde, Meili was no match for her muscle-bound assailant. Armed with a knife, he slashed at her face and body and bludgeoned her with rocks and branches. The sexual assault was brutal and unremitting, both raping and sodomising her. One of her eyes was hanging out of its socket and she had lost 75% of her blood. She was left for dead and was found just before dawn; her body still thrashing around in a paroxysm of death throes.

Her injuries were so severe, a local priest administered the last rites as she was brought into hospital. She was to spend 12 days in a coma before regaining consciousness and beginning a very long, slow journey back toward recovery.

The citizens of New York were incensed; the story was so horrific it made the front pages and TV headlines of almost every Country in the world. The NYPD attributed the attack to a practice known as "wilding" where a gang of feral youths would descend in pack-like formation on vulnerable loners, raping, robbing or assaulting them. Several other attacks had been reported that night and the Police concentrated their efforts on one of these gangs. Reyes himself was briefly interviewed by Police but no one made the connection that he was in fact the assailant.

This was the final straw for New York's newly installed mayor Rudolph Guilliani and he initiated what was to become a model for many other cities around the world. It was to be a policy of zero tolerance.

Undeterred by the furore created by his latest crime, Reyes went on to rape and murder Lourdes Gonzales, a 24-year-old mother of three very young children. They were locked into a room next door in the basement apartment listening to their mother screaming and pleading for her own life and the life of her unborn child. Stabbing her in the face, he insisted that it was either going to be her eyes or her children. He then went on to stab her 7 more times, slashed her across the eyes and raped her at least three times all within earshot of her terrified children. She died three hours after he left.

It later emerged that three days earlier he had raped another young woman, stabbing her and slashing at her eyes and then tried to drown her in the sink. Police have been able to confirm at least 8 other victims who are still alive but physically scarred and emotionally distressed for life.

The Police were able to tie Matias Reyes to the murder of Lourdes Gonzales and the other rapes and he was sentenced to 33 years but there was still no link made to the Meili assault.

AN UNJUST CALLING?

However, in an extraordinary turn of events, Reyes converted to

Christianity and willingly confessed to the Central Park rape. His detailed knowledge of undisclosed facts and a perfect DNA match left no doubt that he was indeed responsible for that attack.

This story is factual and all information has been collated from Police sources quoted in many different newspaper articles that have covered this story. So why am I repeating it in this book? Because, if the current teaching on the hell doctrine is to be believed, **this story appears to show a level of injustice, on the part of God, that absolutely staggers the imagination**. Let me break this down for you piece by piece:

A man goes out and commits crimes against vulnerable, defenseless young women, of such a horrific magnitude that we can barely comprehend it, much less imagine it. Their lives are scarred and ruined by his actions.

A young pregnant mother of three children is brutally slain. **Under THIS doctrine, she is in hell being subjected to eternal torment**.

He, on the other hand, is given the gift of repentance and forgiven of all his sins. He may still be in jail but his conversion means that he now has eternal life to look forward to, as well as blessings in THIS life.

Isn't this obscene? By any definition of fairness and justice, doesn't this make a joke of everything that Christianity is supposed to stand for?

The gift of repentance hasn't been granted to his victims. They're still living day-to-day with what he has done to them. According to this doctrine, if they die before receiving Christ, eternal suffering waits for them as well. In the meantime, their tormentor on Earth will get to enjoy eternal life without ever having received his "just deserts".

Do you see how utterly discredited this whole scenario has become? I have only given you one isolated example from a potential pool of millions upon millions of examples from around the world and throughout man's history. **The Church cannot defend the indefensible. It crumbles at any exposure to real-life situations**. It defies any sense of rational explanation and, as you will shortly see, the Bible itself shreds this ridiculous doctrine to pieces.

At least one attempt has been made to try and rescue a sense of justice from this story and that was that Matias Reyes had a tough upbringing, that he had suffered abuse and neglect. Well **that cannot be used as some kind of excuse to try and justify his actions**. There are thousands of men who have been through similar experiences who have gone on to make a success of their lives without harming anyone. Reyes made no attempt to exercise restraint, **he knew right from wrong**. Why else did he say to his victims that he wanted to put out their eyes so they wouldn't be able to identify him. He was fearful of being caught and that inbred sense of guilt is what defines someone who knows right from wrong. He did what he did because he wanted to.

I am glad, for his sake, that he has found repentance but I can only say that because I know what the implications are. I know what the outcome for his victims will be, but **what I know is derived from Biblical instruction, not from religious superstition** and, by the end of this book, I want you, the reader, to have as thorough a grasp on the truth as I've been given.

The summary on global grace for the whole of mankind was no man-made contrivance. It was a synopsis of the whole Bible and, as we proceed, I will reinforce every point with real-life experience, legitimate scientific conclusion and scriptural insight.

WHAT JUSTICE DEMANDS

So far, you have read one example of what could fairly be assumed as an unfair act on God's part by pardoning the offender rather than his victims. I'm sure you could point to many others but our sense of justice tends to originate from personal experience within a confined set of circumstances. **This creates a myopic view where we don't account for many other factors that affect the outcome of a just decision.**

Any justice system in the world has to allow for a certain degree of vengeance to be built into the system. It's done that way to appease the understandable feelings of hurt, betrayal loss or on-going trauma. **The victim typically demands three things from any justice system:**

1. Punishment for the offender.
2. Restitution for the harm caused.
3. The assurance that said offence will never be repeated.

No justice system can fully satisfy the people it purports to serve unless those 3 elements are in place and are applied equally across all social, religious and ethnic groups. **It must be noted by the reader that these ideals are rarely achieved** and that these ideals are based upon a man-made philosophy that is largely uninformed by scriptural insight.

Punishment for the Offender

How does that work? Well, before we get to that, what about the offence itself? **At what point does an action translate into harm against another person?** Does it begin when someone tells a lie? Does it begin with an act of selfishness or greed that has repercussions way beyond the understanding of the offender? Does it begin when a person fails to live up to his word? Actually, the answer to all 3 questions is YES! But, our justice systems find it difficult to legislate for such personal failings, much less being able to police and prosecute those failings.

The harm that results from these human weaknesses can be difficult to trace back so that blame can be properly apportioned. This points to a significant weakness in any man-made justice system. There is global guilt. **To one degree or another we have all contributed to the suffering on this planet**, either by collusion, apathy or direct action. None of us have clean hands.

It suits human wisdom to draw clear demarcation lines between the offender and the victim. We categorise them as the Perpetrator (the guilty party) and the Victim (the innocent party). **The Perpetrator is defined as someone who inflicts physical or psychological harm upon another.** Some examples would include: A torturer, a rapist, a child abuser, a wife beater, a murderer, a kidnapper, an adulterer, a robber or a burglar. Anyone, who by virtue of greater strength, position or power, causes distress to another who is of a weaker disposition.

VICTIM PERSPECTIVE

Typically, these victims experience loss of self-worth. Their sense of helplessness is greatly increased and they become consumed with mis-trust and fear. Fear, in its turn, breeds a virulent cocktail of hatred, suspicion and despair. **But, most damaging of all, is their all-consuming desire for Vengeance**. The desire for vengeance is like a great big black hole in human nature. It is a bottomless pit that can never be fully satisfied. **It also leads to terrible consequences that go far beyond the initial feelings of hatred towards the perpetrator**. Misery likes company. Pain must be shared. So, this unresolved wound in human experience spreads like a cancer. Bitter words expressed to a loving relative nurtures empathy and outrage in the heart of the relative. This is swiftly followed by accusation and blame that foments hostility and mis-trust. **Now, it isn't just the fault of the perpetrator, it's his family, his neighbourhood, his race, his religion**. Anything connected to him becomes fair game as the desire for vengeance feeds upon itself.

The Bible explains all this. The Bible warns all of us about letting these things get out of hand. The Bible does not come with a list of recommendations that are open to discussion. It tells us about two ways to live: One way leads to life, health, prosperity, peace and happiness; the other way leads to death, sickness, poverty, war and misery. For the most part mankind has chosen the latter. **The consequences don't happen overnight**, they grow and develop until destruction comes suddenly and, if we're not paying attention, unexpectedly.

Who is the enemy of Mankind? Who has deceived the whole world?

A CUNNING PLAN

By tempting people into breaking the planet-wide laws that govern human relationships, Satan has executed his master plan brilliantly.

He turns us against each other by exploiting the weakness of one man by appealing either to his vanity, his personal lusts, his insecurity or his selfishness. The man finds these thoughts appealing and dwells upon them. They become a fantasy and the fantasy is fed until it demands physical satiation. But the real world doesn't allow for this, so now he has to impose his will on the life of another in order to make his fantasy come true. **So the intent of his heart is acted out against another, creating a victim because of the pain caused either directly or indirectly by this man.**

This newly created victim and/or his/her relatives and friends will seek to avenge this wrong-doing by visiting their retribution on his head. If they can't get to him, they'll go after his loved ones. If they're successful, the relatives and friends of the perpetrator (who didn't believe the accusations made against him in the first place) will go after the family and friends of the victim. And so the cycle goes: "An eye for an eye, a tooth for a tooth until the whole world ends up blind and toothless".

Which brings us full circle back to the question: At what point does an action translate into harm against another person? **Answer: Any thought, word or deed that is contrary to the expressed will of God concerning our relationship with Him and our relationship with one another.** Who is guilty of this? Every man and woman that has ever lived, is living now or likely to live in the future. Guilt is universal. Condemnation is universal. Ergo, salvation, if it is to mean anything, will have to be given a chance for universal application.

In the meantime, humanity lives under planet-wide law. This law is like the law of gravity. **It has universal application in the life of every human being.** If we break this law (which all of us, to one degree or another, have done), this law will exact due recompense. No one gets away with anything. Sometimes, that recompense will be accurately interpreted and punished through the various justice systems that exist in the world today.

Most nations have a judicial system that decides whether the accused is guilty or not and then hands down what they consider to be the most appropriate punishment. **Unfortunately, all judicial systems are run by men and women which means they have inherent weaknesses.** First, they cannot read the minds of those accused of a crime and therefore can never be absolutely sure that they have the right man. Also, in order for any judicial system to be effective, there has to be an even-handed application of the law across all social boundaries. But this rarely happens because judgement is being exercised by imperfect men whose own lives are clouded with sin and prejudice. They're also susceptible to influential persons who may wish to corrupt the system through financial favours and unmerited awards.

Then, there's the law itself which is written by imperfect men and varies from nation to nation and culture to culture. **These statutes tend to reflect the attitudes, beliefs and priorities of the incumbent ruling structure which does not always reflect the needs and best interests of the people they purport to govern.** Unfortunately, this tends to lead to miscarriages of justice for a large proportion of people. This subject is dealt with in more detail in my book: *Exposing the Curse.*

WHEN KARMA-HEADS PREVAIL

But injustice is also perceived to occur when someone DOESN'T appear to be punished for their offence. Even the most dedicated Law enforcement official will tell you that approximately **70% of crimes against the person are never prosecuted**; either through lack of evidence, reluctant witnesses or the inability to accurately identify the offender. So do they get away with it? Some argue in favour of the Karmic solution which is **the belief that what goes around will come around. That you'll reap what you sow:** "Do good unto others as you would like them to do to you and you'll enjoy a good life. Do evil, bad or hurtful things to other people and all that bad Karma will come back and haunt you". Sounds good right? Surely that all makes sense. In fact, some of those quotes originate from the Bible and yes, there is a lot of truth in them, BUT NOT THE WHOLE TRUTH . . .

DIVINE SURVEILLANCE

Did you know that God tells us that every thought, word and deed, by every human being in the world, is recorded? That means that in the last 24 hours, every word that has been spoken by every human being on the planet; that's 7 billion people speaking an average of 3,000 words (that's twenty one trillion words) is now down on record. How many thoughts have you had in the last 24 hours? What have you physically done in the last 24 hours? Now multiply that by the number of days that you've been alive on this Earth. Now multiply that figure by the number of people that have lived since Adam and Eve, are living now and will live in the future . . .

Everything is known, EVERYTHING! And this Planet-wide law is adjudicating on every thought, word and action of every human being. No one is getting away with anything. **All our interactions are known, all our schemes and plans are known.** Have you ever heard the following great big fat lies:

1. It's just a matter of luck.
2. You were in the wrong place at the wrong time.
3. Life is just a lottery.
4. You were born lucky.
5. We're all just puppets on a string.

We have world-class scientists today who have uncovered the most intricate of designs at a sub-cellular level in the three major fields of Biology, Physics and Chemistry. That's just the physical world around us. With all their insights they've barely scratched the surface of human beings. We're a fearsomely complex design of creation. Everyone of us unique.

There are no accidents, there are no "unforeseen" events, there are no issues of "blind chance". But take an event such as an outbreak of cancer. Medical researchers are always looking for a single common denominator to explain the formation of a particular type of cancer. This is an overly simplistic approach. It would be a frightfully complex thing to do but if it were possible to access the records showing all the thoughts, words and deeds of the infected individual from the time he became cognisant, then add in generational factors of condemnation woven into his DNA, **it may be possible to pin-point the time that his fate was sealed by the adjudication that led to this illness**.

Suppose a bomb goes off and kills 20 people. They're terminated so they're okay, but their relatives are not. They go on living with the fall-out of their loss. Same with the injured. **Even the extent of the injury has a pre-determined element, as does the rate of recovery**. Yet there is surely nothing more random than an explosion. Anyway, you get the idea. We are in very deep territory here but I'm just trying to illustrate **how utterly bound up our lives are with super-natural design**. I'm also attempting to demonstrate just how deeply human beings have been deceived by constantly seeking secular solutions to spiritual problems.

We're on deep background here but my point is that all those strange instructions that Jesus gave to His disciples concerning matters of judgement and forgiveness were given to free up the solution of grace as being the answer to all of mankind's problems. Later on in this book we'll be looking at the issue of malnutrition to the point of starvation that currently exists in many parts of the Christian church today.

A DECEPTION OF GLOBAL MAGNITUDE

Let me close out this issue of vengeance with this crucial summation. In pursuing vengeance against the perpetrator, whether directly or through an imperfect justice system, the victim is helping to propagate evil by this obsession for revenge. As long as the victim retains ownership of this desire, the perpetrator will never experience repentance and is PROTECTED from the consequences due to him. His crimes will continue to prosper because the victim refuses to hand the matter over to God.

Even some Christians are guilty of this and it's one of the reasons why prayers go unanswered. Why do so many people refuse to hand the matter over to God? Because of a massive deception in the way that humanity thinks.

Whatever the offender has done to cause this desire for vengeance in the victim, be aware of this one crucial fact. **The desire for vengeance is itself an extremely powerful deception. The victim does NOT want vengeance. The victim's true desire is that this offence had never happened in the first place**. Is that possible? If a loved one has died, you will definitely see her again. If the victim has suffered permanent injury, she can be completely healed. Hurt feelings can be replaced with a peace that surpasses all understanding. All this requires Pastoral counseling and instruction that must originate from the Bible and also needs informed intercession on her behalf. For Christians, this is more clearly explained in my book: *Miraculous Healing for the Church*.

Restitution for the Harm Caused

We've already touched briefly on this but let's look at human solutions first. The issue of compensation, as it relates to: real or perceived hurt, betrayal, loss or on-going trauma, is played out in civil court actions all over the world. A monetary award is provided, based on the suffering or loss involved. It doesn't change what has happened but it provides the victim with a sense of compensation for what they've been through.

MONEY FOR NOTHING

The trouble is, this can be taken too far **where victims can assume a sense of entitlement**, where lessons, rather than being learned, are lost in a system that doesn't want to recognise that **judgement on that life has taken place**.

Let me give you an example: A young boy openly flouts the instruction from his dad NOT to play soccer in a busy street and gets run over by a car. He ends up badly injured and the driver ends up in Court. The wheels of "justice" turn and the driver's insurance provider pays out a monetary award to cover medical costs and an award to compensate for pain and suffering. The boy recovers and, with all this extra money, the dad decides to take the whole family to Disneyland and buys the boy a new bike. **But the issue of gross disobedience on the part of his son has still not been dealt with**. So what has the boy learned from this? The driver was at fault. The boy didn't do anything wrong. He was entitled to compensation. His dad ran to protect and comfort him when he got hurt. So the boy has shown no contrition and the dad refuses to assign blame and discipline him appropriately and, consequently, this boy's way of thinking has been corrupted.

This is happening all over the place. **Rather than examine all the potential causes that led up to the suffering of a victim, the priority is now given over to ignoring the potential lessons**, avoiding the repentance that should flow from that and, instead, providing restitution before it's been earned.

UNFORGIVEN

When the apartheid system in South Africa was formally abandoned in 1994, the reformist, Nelson Mandela, was elected as President. In an effort to minimise acts of retribution for all the hurts committed during the apartheid years, it was decided to set up a TRUTH AND RECONCILIATION COMMISSION. Victims would recount their experiences in the presence of their tormentors who would, in turn, express their regret and ask for forgiveness and amnesty.

This form of **restorative justice**, as it was known, was based on the idea of confession and forgiveness leading to reconciliation. It was endorsed by religious leaders and social and political reformers across the world and hailed as a great leap forward in the quest for world peace.

It would be churlish to criticise such efforts, but there was considerable scepticism expressed about its effectiveness. Not least because **the hoped-for "peace dividend" never really materialised.** White farmers were murdered, inter-tribal conflict increased and family abuse and poverty exploded. Misery and pain was compounded because victims cannot forgive from their own resources. They need super-natural help. **The victim has to be reconciled to God FIRST, then he/she can deal with the forgiveness process, as it's outlined in the Bible.** The restorative-justice-program sought to achieve a good outcome but they tried to do it by circumventing our Creator. Nice try, but it was doomed to failure because it plays into the hands of our enemy who wants to keep Mankind separated from God.

So the victims of apartheid still have their injuries, disablements, family break-downs, poverty, addictions, mental disorders. **The healing just hasn't materialised for many of those people**. This is the problem with man-made solutions to justice. Victims will only get FULL RESTITUTION when the process of ACCEPTANCE, ACCOUNTABILITY and DIVINELY-INSPIRED FORGIVENESS have been fully accomplished and that can only be achieved through Jesus Christ.

We must never forget that **the Bible teaches us to identify the causes behind every event**. It requires self-examination. It requires examination of circumstances, behaviour, genetic traits, family and community culpability. It's that taking of personal responsibility that leads to appropriate contrition, then repentance which, **if genuine, will swiftly lead to generous restitution**; often above and beyond anything that could be awarded by a Court of Law. We cannot side-step or rush this process and yes, it is a process. It won't happen overnight but **the end result will be a life transformed by admitting error, taking responsibility and making corrections to lifestyle and behaviour**. This process truly transforms the life of the victim and opens them up to all manner of blessings and restitution that really means something.

The Assurance that Said Offence Will Never Be Repeated

It's fair to say that anyone who has ever been a victim of physical violence will experience what psychologists call paranoia. The idea that everyone is a potential assailant, that any trust or feeling of security has been completely undermined. If the victim is religious, her faith in God, in terms of protection, has been shot to pieces. If the victim placed her faith in her husband, her extended family, the Police, kindness of a stranger; all that has now gone.

She feels let down, abandoned and incredibly vulnerable. Despite the assurances of friends and relatives she cannot extract a firm or sure promise from anyone that this will never happen again.

The justice system will seek to capture and incarcerate the perpetrator. They may be successful but the assurances that the victim is really after just doesn't exist in any justice system anywhere in the world.

So let's take a look at her worldly options:

Let's start with Law Enforcement:

The Police service exist to protect and serve the public by enforcing laws that have been enacted Locally, Regionally or Nationally. Their presence on the street helps to deter criminal activity. The trouble is, **the Police are not clairvoyant**. They cannot read minds. They don't know when or where a murderer, rapist, robber or assailant will strike next, or who they will strike. Ninety percent of the time, the Police will show up **after the event**. This isn't a criticism, it's simply a fact of life. Unfortunately, by then, **the damage has been done** and nothing the Police can do will reverse that fact.

Also, most sexual and physical assaults take place in the home and a fairly reliable statistic indicates that less than 10% of those are ever reported to the authorities. In some countries that figure is less than one percent. This tends to increase public perception that justice is not being done, that the delegated authorities are unable to handle the scale of social problems that are besetting most nations today. So, **priorities tend to be skewed toward preventing escalation**, keeping a lid on a powder keg that's getting set to explode.

This means dealing with the ever present threat of vigilantism, where people give in to the impulse of taking the law into their own hands. This is happening more and more, especially in the younger generation. More and more, our young people prefer to deal with their conflicts in-house which is giving rise to greater levels of crime and revenge attacks. Virtually all these problems can be traced back to the breakdown of family life and the abandoning of responsibility by so many feckless fathers. **Nations are finding that they can't put the family back together**, so they enact new laws to try and deal with some of the social consequences. Again, this helps to keep a lid on things but it doesn't resolve the core problems. Also, **these new regulations have the unintended consequence of undermining many of the freedoms that people in the West have come to cherish** and, in turn, this increases tension between the citizen and the governing authorities. (See: *Exposing the Curse*).

Life is getting more dangerous, more unstable, more unpredictable. Law enforcement officials may desire to "Protect and Serve" but **they can't be everywhere at once.** So where does this leave our victim who is seeking the reassurance that she won't be attacked again? **No such**

assurance can be given, which consequently brings us to the thorny subject of Self Defense.

DEFEND AND PROTECT

Nature teaches us that self-defense is a basic instinct inherent in all creatures that are open to attack from predators. This is especially true of the human race. **We don't trust each other, that's why we have military forces** that are trained and equipped to defend national populations. That instinct also exists on a personal level. If you attack me, threaten my loved ones or attempt to steal my stuff, I'm going to defend myself.

Our laws, for the most part, respect that right. The trouble is, there are growing instances where the law is being used to prosecute citizens and law enforcement officials for defending themselves using deadly force. This is very confusing to a lot of people as **it's the assailant who puts himself in the position of exposure to deadly force**. He provoked it, he incited it, he attacked first. He drew first blood, he threatened, he invaded. If the right to use proportionate or deadly force to protect ourselves from a predator is undermined by restrictions in the law, **the citizen will instinctively start regarding the law as a threat to himself**, his loved ones and his property. This will diminish his respect for the law and those who enforce it. This is a dangerous threat to the stability of any free society as the sense of community will be lost.

The other relevant issue is **the MEANS of self defense**. Going back to our analogy from nature, we can see that creatures are armed with the means to deter the most likely of predators that target their particular species. Certain insects have stings and poisons. Some animals have horns or claws and teeth. Some protect themselves with speed and flight or blending into their surroundings like the chameleon. Some run in packs or use each other to create a united force that deters their predators.

But imagine a situation where nature de-claws a lioness after she's given birth to her cubs or takes the stings away from bees after they've built their hive. The natural world is hostile and **these creatures wouldn't last long if they were denied an appropriate means of self-defense**. Likewise, human beings need an equaliser to deter potential predators from targetting them. For instance, a 5 foot tall, 60 pound female will not stand much of a chance against a 6 foot tall, 200 pound man that is high on crack and determined to harm her.

THE PRINCIPLE OF DETERRENCE

Her most effective deterrent is to arm herself with a handgun and be thoroughly trained in its use as a deterrent or, if necessary, as a means of deadly force.

In a Country like the United States of America, the right to bear arms has been enshrined in the Constitution since its inception. **What has been really surprising is the lengths that many Americans have had to go to to uphold those rights.** They fight a constant battle to protect themselves against legal encroachments that seek to undermine their right to self-defense. Who are their protagonists and why are they so determined to dis-arm law-abiding, family-orientated, stable citizens? **What are their arguments, what is their agenda?**

Before we can answer that, we have to turn the spotlight on the United Kingdom of Great Britain. The Country of my birth has been the focus of anti-gun groups as **the ideal example of a peaceful, unarmed society**. But is it?

About 300 years ago Britain kick-started the industrial revolution and people moved from working in the fields to living and working in the cities. Poverty and crime were rampant and in London in the 1800s, wealthy merchants decided to implement the ideas of Robert Peel and set up the world's first police force. Back then, the UK was riven with class and privilege and the idea of equality and social mobility was an alien concept. The upper class wanted to hold onto their wealth and status and used laws and the Police to enforce the ban of weapons being held by those of a lower rank. Britain never had a Second Amendment. The right to bear arms has never been granted to the wider population but criminals never really took advantage of what this vulnerability could mean to them. There is a very good reason for this and we will look at that in a moment.

After the Second World War, many soldiers, returning from the front lines, brought guns and ammunition back with them. They were stored in attics or framed in display cabinets and kept as trophies of a bygone era. These weapons were rarely used in cases of self-defense because the nation was largely at peace with itself. So, for the most part, they sat there and gathered dust. The authorities broadly knew of their existence but there was no perceived threat to law and order, so no action was taken to recover them. Even the industrial turbulence of the '70s brought no threat of armed insurrection. Clashes between protesters and the Police were confined to stone-throwing and baton charges. All in all there was a very good balanced relationship between law enforcement and the citizen.

THE DUNBLANE TRAGEDY

But all that suddenly changed on the morning of Wednesday 13th March 1996.

On a cold Spring morning in the picturesque village of Dunblane near Stirling in Scotland, mothers hurriedly prepared their 5 and 6 year old children for school. The children chattered aimlessly about painting projects while their mothers packed lunch pails with sandwiches and crisps before hurrying them out the door. After dropping them off, the mothers went off to do their respective chores or hurried off to work in confident expectation that they would see their little ones straight after school. As they made mental notes about what they would prepare for dinner, a 43-year-old single man named Thomas Hamilton had something infinitely more sinister in mind.

For a long time Hamilton had been nursing grudges against a system that he believed had been persecuting him. A former scout and youth club leader, he believed his calling was to mentor children but his methods were often criticized and led to complaints from parents which were subsequently referred to Police and other authorities. His paranoia grew; believing he had been branded as a pervert whenever he was taunted by his former charges and he became more and more isolated. With no career, no friends and no prospects he fuelled his frustrations with vengeful fantasies. How could he best hurt those who had destroyed his life? The answer grew clearer.

Looking like just another parent, Hamilton entered the Dunblane Primary School and followed the sound of excited children to the School's gymnasium. Armed with two semi-automatic pistols and two Smith and Wesson revolvers and over 700 rounds of ammunition, he began firing as soon as he entered the gym. Over the next three to five minutes of indiscriminate shooting, firing approximately 105 bullets, he shot and killed one teacher and fifteen children. A further 12 children and two teachers had also been shot and injured. One child later died in hospital. At this point Hamilton turned the gun on himself.

The shocked silence that followed was interrupted only by the sound of running footsteps as other teachers, responding to the shooting and screaming sounds, entered the gym to investigate the cause of all this mayhem. The sight that greeted their eyes turned them to stone . . .

Within minutes emergency services were on the scene. Paramedics worked feverishly to stabilise the wounded. Police officers secured the scene and then the media arrived en masse. News of the Dunblane school massacre was flashed around the world; many viewers and even some of the reporters reduced to tears unable to take in the awful events that had just transpired. Within the town itself, as news of the tragedy spread, terrified parents, in a state of shock and disbelief, congregated outside the school pleading to know where their children were. The cameras caught the tearful scenes as relieved parents were reunited with their confused offspring but they also brought into focus parents whose cries of despair were heard as Police ushered them toward waiting vehicles.

The grieving process was to take months. The funerals, the memorial services, the Royal visits, the ritualistic demolition of the gymnasium, the absolute avalanche of condolence messages, flowers and gifts that poured in from throughout the world. The subsequent police investigation would tie off with Thomas Hamilton. No other party was involved. So there would be no prosecution, no trial and, for bereaved parents, no sense of closure. However, the four guns used in the murder of these children were legally held. The law was at fault. If all handguns were made illegal then this tragedy could have been averted. In spite of the illogical nature of such an argument, the media happily took up the cause. They had their scapegoat. Feeding off the emotions of a shocked public, the snowdrop campaign was formed and hundreds of thousands of signatures were collected across the UK. The petitions were presented to the British Government and the media practically dared the MPs to rule any other way than for the complete ban on all legally-held handguns in the UK.

THE GUN-BLAME TRAVESTY

Under enormous media-fuelled pressure, they capitulated and signed into law some of the most aggressive anti-gun legislation the world has ever seen. An amnesty was declared for the surrender of all unlicensed weapons and **the myth was firmly established that the law was at fault, that all gun owners were potential murderers** and that the tragedy of Dunblane could have been averted had these conditions existed prior to the Spring of 1996.

Many European nations sought to follow Britain's lead by toughening up their own anti-gun legislation. Though the snowdrop campaign met stiff resistance when it sought to spread its message to America, as it encountered tough questions about the viability and usefulness of such a move.

The British position has since been made untenable by the murder of toddlers in a Belgian nursery by a knife-wielding maniac. Or the slashing and stabbing of little children in play-schools and nurseries across China. **The absence of guns does not make a society safer**. In fact, if women, including primary school teachers, were allowed to possess and carry handguns they could have successfully defended the children in their care and minimised the casualties involved.

Two years before the Dunblane tragedy, **one million Tutsis, including women and children, were slaughtered in Rwanda by Hutu men wielding machetes and clubs**. Does anyone seriously believe that if machetes and clubs had been banned that the slaughter would never have taken place? It's a ridiculous proposition that no one would ever take seriously.

Knee-jerk reaction is not a sound basis for good law-making. As the Bible makes perfectly clear, any act of murder, cruelty, greed or selfishness is a consequence of an unsound mind. We cannot legislate against such defective thinking. **If someone is heart-set upon a course of action designed to harm another, he will find a way to fulfill it**. Take away his gun, he'll use a knife. Take away his knife, he'll use a club, a brick, poison, his fists, his car. Against such tenacious determination, **the only recourse is deterrent**. Law enforcement can only do so much. They're not clairvoyant. They don't know who, where, how or when the assailant will strike next. So the potential victims (the public) should be granted both the legal right AND the means to protect themselves from such an eventuality. **With the right framework, working in full cooperation with the authorities, any Country can successfully incorporate such a policy within their governing structure**.

A DEFENSIVE AMENDMENT

I am not a campaigner for such an issue but if a nation, such as the United Kingdom of Great Britain chose to take a lead on this and show the rest of the world how a policy like this could be implemented; I would make the following recommendations:

1. Clarify the law so that the principle of self-defense and proportionality can be clearly stated.
2. Gun ownership should be limited to handguns and only made available to those who would have to satisfy the following criteria:
   a) No one under the age of 21 would be allowed to own a gun.
   b) No one with a criminal record that involves acts of violence, threats or intimidation would be allowed to own a gun.
   c) No one with a history of, or under the influence from, alcohol or drug abuse or any form of legal mind-altering drug or intoxication would be allowed to own a gun.
   d) No one with a history of deceit, theft, dishonesty, lying or deception would be allowed to own a gun.

So this would discount approximately one third of the population from enjoying this privilege and ensure the good behaviour of all gun owners who would otherwise lose the right to own a gun if they offended under any of these categories.

Like a suspended driving license, offenders would have to demonstrate a period of responsibility, under all these categories, before the right to gun ownership could be reinstated. This period should be 5 years.

In addition to all the above, all potential gun owners would have to submit to a psychiatric test that would be designed to flag up areas of concern. As I understand it, Police Officers in the UK who are authorised to carry firearms, are already subjected to these tests. The same standard should be applied to citizens.

Having got this far, the next stage would be COMPULSORY training, which the applicant would have to pay for. This training should be carried out by qualified ex-servicemen and women who would demonstrate all aspects of safety and effective use of the weapon in a wide variety of situations. Ex-police officers would also be involved who would demonstrate how a citizen should safely respond in any situation where a law enforcement official might pull them over in a motor vehicle or seek to interview them at home. Ex-civil servants would be a good source of recruitment for training applicants in their understanding and obligations under the law. All these professionals would be involved in these training classes all over the Country and each profession would oversee the testing of the applicant to ensure their full accreditation as a responsible gun owner. Only then would the Home Office grant a license.

The Police would then have all the gun-owners details on file, his/her accreditation, the make, model and serial number of his/her weapon and the ballistics match.

As well as all the employment this would create for the professionals, there would also be room for advanced training, shooting ranges and a COMPULSORY one-day refresher course every year for all gun owners. In addition to that would be the manufacture of the weapons themselves. Again, the UK would have to take the lead by manufacturing hand-guns that could only be used by the owner. This would require advanced design rendering the weapon useless in the hands of another. It's quite achievable once you create a market for it. Having set the model legislation, restrictions, training and equipment, the UK would have a viable export that would find favour in every democratic country in the world and silence those critics whose horror of guns does not embrace any sense of reality.

In the event that a fully accredited gun owner is involved in a shooting; fatal or otherwise. The Police would initiate an investigation to determine whether or not this was self-defense. The procedures adopted would parallel those of an "officer-involved-shooting". Fairness, even-handedness, same rules for everyone. The basis for good government the world over.

PROTECTIVE PRECAUTIONS

My readers are probably surprised that a Christian writer would endorse such views. Some of my Christian readers may be uncomfortable that I am not proclaiming a more peaceful approach; such as beating swords into ploughshares. Well a time will come when that will be possible, but it isn't going to happen before Christ comes back. In the meantime, the people of this world have to take precautions to safeguard themselves and their loved ones. The State can only do so much, everything else is down to the individual and their community.

Remember, this subject began with the question: HOW DO YOU PROVIDE THE ASSURANCE THAT SAID OFFENCE WILL NEVER BE REPEATED? The answer is: **Take personal responsibility for your safety which includes harnessing the right to self-defense**. We do that as a nation through our armed forces. We seek to do that as a community through our Police service, now we need to look at the issue of doing that on a personal and family level through safe and responsible training and law-abiding gun ownership.

Criminals will always disregard the law. **No amount of legislation will deter a hardened criminal**. But a well-trained, armed populace is a significant deterrent to all manner of criminal activity. Some obvious examples are the modern state of Israel and Switzerland. But it has worked there for all the reasons given above. The United States of America however, is not the best example because of their lack of uniformity. Their laws are very confusing and ad-hoc and unevenly applied. They also embrace an adversarial approach to the issues of self-defense that deny cool, calm, rational reasoning on either side of the debate.

Earlier, I referred to the fact that criminals, operating in Britain, never really took full advantage of the "vulnerability" of our unarmed citizens by arming themselves. This wasn't because they couldn't get access to guns, this was because of the unseen protective veil that covered the British people. Call it rugged common sense. Call it a sense of righteousness, fair-play. An inherent sense of justice and personal responsibility. Even those of a criminal disposition were aware of it, even if they didn't know how to articulate it, which helped dissuade them from taking advantage of our unarmed state. The UK had a strong sense of destiny (note the past tense). Our Judaeo-Christian heritage meant something even if it wasn't always fully embraced by its people. Call it the hand of God over our nation.

Even before the second world war, Hitler and his henchmen were reluctant to go to war against Britain. They may not have liked us but there was a respect, even an admiration for its peoples and its institutions. Unfortunately, against our better judgement, we have chosen to disregard the heritage bequeathed to us by our forbears and we've embraced a secular agenda on many issues (some of which are detailed in the book *Exposing the Curse*) that have built a wall between us and the One who has watched over us.

So, **armed or not, we face a much more dangerous and uncertain**

future than we had before. So we need to re-think our traditional position on self-defense.

LIVE BY THE SHIELD

What about the Biblical position for Christians when it comes to self-defense? When the disciples walked around with Jesus, some of them carried swords and knives. Jesus never rebuked them for that. In fact, **the only recorded rebuke from Jesus about the use of a weapon was when Peter cut off the ear of the High Priest** when he came to arrest Jesus in Gethsemene. Jesus said that those who live by the sword will die by the sword. But we have to remember that Peter committed an illegal act. The party coming to arrest Jesus were doing so under a legal warrant. **The warrant may have been unjustified but the authority of the High Priest and the rest of the party was genuine**. Peter defied that authority and assaulted an officer of the law. If Jesus hadn't healed the ear of the High Priest, Peter could have been legally arrested and charged. Peter showed a disrespect and contempt for the law by his action. Admittedly, **he did this to defend Jesus but Jesus never gave him any such instruction**. So he wasn't living by the Word of God, or acting on the instruction of Jesus or by the law of the land. He acted presumptuously. In that moment, he was living by the sword. **He was feeding off his emotions**. He had cast off restraint and acted with a sense of vengeance. It was in that context that Jesus rebuked him.

So where does that leave Christians? We're instructed to overcome evil with good, not to put a cap in their ass. If someone compels us to walk one mile, we happily walk two. We pray for our enemies and do good to those who take advantage of us. We respect the law; even if it's unjust and works against us. We hold all men and women in high regard and don't repay evil for evil. **So does this mean that we become a doormat for every mugger, rapist, murderer, child molester and assailant that comes our way?** No it doesn't. Jesus was never intimidated by every-day criminals. He had Spiritual authority and

He knew how to use it. He saw beyond the physical body and instead addressed the spirit behind it. That takes knowledge, faith, maturity and experience to do that. For all other Christians, they need to stay close to God and implement His ways in their lives. That way, they can have confidence in God's promises of protection for themselves and their loved ones.

Should Christians own guns? Sure, why not? If anyone can be trusted with gun ownership there's surely no one better suited than a law-abiding, God-fearing Christian. **We can also be trusted with knives, baseball bats and bricks as well**, because the intent of our heart is for good and not evil. What about using a gun for self-defense? The simple answer is: We shouldn't have to. All things being equal, if we are obedient to all of Christ's teachings in the New Covenant, a situation like the ones described should never arise.

NO MINISTRY FOR THE FEARFUL

What about martyrdom? Now we're talking about ministry. Ministry is an act of service done on behalf of Jesus Christ which may, or may not, include declarations of faith and Biblical teaching to unbelievers. **This work sometimes attracts violent opposition which may or may not result in the violent death of the preacher**. That may be what the future holds for some of us and self-defense would actually defeat the object of what God is seeking to teach His people through us. The simple point is this: If, as a Christian, we're more concerned about preserving our physical lives than we are about serving God in ministry, then we're not yet ready for ministry, because we'll end up compromising what God is seeking to do through us. **We cannot adopt the "Rambo" solution to persecution**. That's the world's way and in the end it doesn't really work.

WHEN CHRISTIANS "LOSE" DIVINE PROTECTION

Suppose a Christian, who is still young in the faith and not yet in ministry, is violently assaulted and feels that she can no longer trust God with her protection?

This is a very good question and there are instances where this has actually happened. It sounds like a callous thing to say but nothing happens in a vacumn. **There is a cause for every effect and God NEVER breaks His Word.** Outside of ministry there is only one way that something like this can happen. In some way the victim has moved away from grace and placed herself back under the law. How can that happen? The reader will need to read my two previous books: "Miraculous Healing for the Church" and "Exposing The Curse" for a more detailed explanation. But basically it boils down to one of two things. The victim has continued doing something that she has been warned about several times in the past but chose to ignore . . . OR . . . The victim has continuously ignored instructions about what she was supposed to DO and chose not to do it. **It sounds like harsh judgement but it applies to all of us.** We have to be diligent to make our calling and election sure. We should be wary of thinking we're in right-standing with God when the opposite may be true. All the instruction we need is in the Bible and Bible-based books like the two already mentioned.

The way back for a Christian who finds him or herself in that position is clearly explained in my book: *Miraculous Healing for the Church.*

PART NINE

The Biblical Case for Global Grace

Global grace is all about the extraordinary revelation of life after death for everyone!

For every human being, the fear of death is an every-day reality. We're all affected by it, it affects our decisions, it's the source of our greatest distress.

It isn't just the fear of death itself but what happens afterwards. The great unknown. For centuries the Christian Church has taught that Hell waits for those who have done evil and haven't repented and Heaven is the reward for those who do good and honour God with their lives.

So why is it that the Bible tells a very different story?

We reveal a mysterious code hidden in ancient scriptures that identifies God's original plan of redemption. We are also about to examine every scripture that has ever been used to try and prop up the existing theory of Heaven and Hell theology.

Here is a very brief outline of the main holy days and feasts that reveal God's ultimate plan of salvation for the whole of mankind.

There are many online studies that are freely available for all bible students who desire to know more about this. **but I must caution my readers to exercise due diligence by allowing scripture to interpret scripture and be careful of man-made opinions . . .**

The 7 Holy Days/Feasts of Leviticus 23

Passover – sacrifice of the Lamb who was slain from the foundation of the world.

Feast of Unleavened Bread – pictures the suffering Christ who took all our sins and their consequences upon Himself. (*see*: http://bible-truth.org/feasts-unleavenbread.html) Christians should note that whenever they celebrate Communion, it should be done with unleavened bread. As leaven (yeast) represents sin. So using ordinary bread displays an ignorance of scripture and God's plan of salvation that hurts the church and can make us ineffective.

Pentecost – also described as the "feast-of-**first**-fruits" or the Spring Harvest. The Holy Spirit is given to the Church which represents the Bride of Christ.

Feast of Trumpets – refers to the First resurrection (rapture) of the Saints. (*see*: http://bible-truth.org/Feasts-Trumpets.html). Many believe that this was the actual day of Christ's birth.

Atonement – the Final Judgement on this world's systems, a period of mourning and affliction that culminates with the binding of Satan and the physical return of Jesus Christ to planet Earth.

Feast of Tabernacles – the Millennial reign of Jesus Christ with the Saints over what's left of the world's population. This will be a time of great restoration.

Last Great Day – or the main harvest that foreshadows the resurrection of The Rest Of The Dead.

Isaiah 65:20-25: 100 year judgement for the whole of humanity. He who is still a sinner at 100 years old will be burned up and lost for ever. Those who have learned their lesson and developed the humility of a child will be transformed at the same moment.

Space prevents me from sharing a much more detailed study of the scriptures which illuminate the significance that these Holy Days/Feasts have in prophecy. Numerous Jewish and Christian scholars have uncovered allusions to them in their studies. No one scholar has the full interpretation. Each has built on the work of others.

So look them up and check the actual scriptures they refer to and see how the scriptures interpret one another.

The primary purpose of my work is to deal with the HELL DOCTRINE and the scriptural analysis for that.

The Christian message is all about being saved. But saved from what? Hell? **Yes, hell on earth, the hell humanity has helped create on earth**. The hell of separation from God in this life. The hell that the bible describes in such great detail in every book in the bible. The hell of our sins and their consequences which we see all around us:

Galatians 1

³Grace to you and peace from God the Father and our Lord Jesus Christ,
*⁴who gave Himself for our sins, **that He might deliver us from this present evil age**, according to the will of our God and Father,*

Deliver us from a future hell? No!

Deliver us from this **present** evil age, this means deliverance from addictions, poverty, illness, family troubles, violence, abuse.

Make no mistake, hell is real. It's not fictitious, it **is** a place of torture, of misery, of pain and horror. The bible tells us exactly where it is and who created it . . .

Romans 8

[19]*For the earnest expectation of the creation eagerly waits for the revealing of the sons of God.*
[20]*For the creation was subjected to futility, not willingly, but because of Him who subjected it in hope;*
[21]*because the creation itself also will be delivered from the bondage of corruption into the glorious liberty of the children of God.*
[22]*For we know that the whole creation groans and labors with birth pangs together until now.*

Salvation from all these troubles can only be found in Christ. But only when we repent and turn to Him and put our trust in Him and when we agree to be instructed by Him so that he can lead us out of the dark and hopeless situation we find ourselves in and into His marvelous light.

The greatest insult against Jesus Christ that has ever been committed is the traditional hell doctrine.

This is a doctrine of demons. All world religions embrace it because the demonic realm want human beings to understand what life is like for them and share their fear and misery about their future fate. But Jesus changed that defeatist, deceptive thinking by giving us good news about the kingdom of God that entered the world, through the life of Jesus, and is still here among his modern-day disciples

Make no mistake, the following is a major bible study that requires someone with extensive knowledge of the whole bible to conduct it and answer questions. Most of the scriptures are illuminated by the context of surrounding verses

Evidence from the Scriptures

The current teaching on hell depends a great deal on the correct interpretation of the Hebrew word SHEOL, which is also translated HADES in the Greek language; from which the word hell is derived.

The word hell, in the Old Testament, is always a translation of the Hebrew word *Sheol*, which occurs sixty-four times, and is rendered "hell" thirty-two times, "grave" twenty-nine times, and "pit" three times.

The word Hell, in the New Testament, is always a translation of either the Greek word HADES (which means exactly the same as Sheol) and occurs eleven times, or the Greek word Gehenna which appears twelve times, or the Greek word Tartarus which appears once.

SHEOL/HADES is an all-inclusive term that describes life on Earth for all human beings who are disconnected from God. It does NOT refer to a future time beyond death. To prove this, we are going to look at every scripture that contains these words and every scripture used by the Church to support the current traditional doctrine. I urge all my readers to look up these scriptures in their OWN Bible and double-check every assertion made.

DEFINITION OF SHEOL/HADES

The primary meaning is, *the place or state of the dead*. it makes no reference to a place of endless torment after death.

SHEOL/HADES is variously described as:

A state of Hopelessness – Living without hope of Eternal Life or
    anything else
A state of suffering
A state of LIVING death
A state of mourning
A state of anxiety
A state of deception
A state of anguish
Worrying, having no faith
A state of fear
Trouble in the flesh
Subject to violence
Subject to temptation
Subject to deceit
No hope beyond the grave
The inability to comprehend true reality (spiritual blindness)
A natural hostility to the truth of God's Word (spiritual deafness)

Sheol/Hades, or hell, is the way of living death, separated from
God. **It is a one-word description that defines life on Earth, as
it presently is**. It does not allude to something beyond the grave.
It refers to our present condition, our fallen nature, our road to
destruction.

SCRIPTURE REFERENCES
FOR HELL (SHEOL) IN THE OLD TESTAMENT

We begin our scriptural analysis by starting with the earliest references
to Sheol, (as hell) in the bible, and continue through to the end of the
Old Testament:

Deuteronomy 32:22

> *For a fire is kindled by my anger, And shall burn to the lowest hell; SHEOL It shall consume the earth with her increase, And set on fire the foundations of the mountains.*(refers to nations and the deceitful foundations they're built on.)

Read the context which is Judgement. The allusion to hell can be safely interpreted as a future event, especially because of verse 21 and in Revelation's lake of fire and the Final Judgement of all the wicked.

Also remember this was Moses' last speech to the children of Israel before his death, so we should not be surprised that God included some end time prophecy in his remarks.

2 Chronicles 33:20

Manasseh rested with his fathers and was buried . . .

He Dies and Amon Succeeds Him (verses 20, 21). *Manasseh slept with his fathers . . .*

Why doesn't the bible say that Manasseh and other evil kings and people went to Sheol or hell or lake of fire? It just states that they rested, died or slept. The bible does not contradict itself, no one has gone to some place of eternal torment. We cannot teach such a bald-faced lie and deception. This work is a quest for the truth . . .

Psalms 9:17

> *The wicked shall be turned into hell, SHEOL, and all the nations that forget God.*

Sheol typically is translated as the grave, barred with gates, cut off from real life. There is no hope there. The inference is God's judgement awaits the wicked. He will turn His face away. There will be no help, His presence will not be there to save them from the consequences of their actions. Their hopeless, miserable state will finally end in death.

Note that death comes to us all regardless of how we live, so for God to specifically use the word Sheol as a consequence for the wicked cannot refer just to the grave, because we all go to the grave. This must refer to the living state of death referred to by Moses when he encouraged his people to choose life and not choose the way of death or terrible consequences in the here and now.

Sin upon sin, trespass upon trespass, error upon error. Like a whirlpool increasing in intensity, evil begets evil, just as dog begets dog until the whole planet is consumed by the consequences of sin.

And it always begins the same way; refusing to acknowledge our Creator and learn and adopt His ways and His priorities. That spirit of rebellion creates a life that turns into a hellish (Sheol) existence.

Psalms 55:15

> Let death seize them; Let them go down alive into hell, SHEOL For wickedness is in their dwellings and among them.

Psalms 55:15 again, taken from The Message *translation*

> Haul my betrayers off alive to hell – let them experience the horror, let them feel every desolate detail of a damned life.

Given the context of this chapter, *The Message* is most appropriate. It is also closely aligned with false Christians who disturb the "love feasts" of the children of God by their betrayal not just to the Church but to the people of this world with their deceptive teachings and practices.

Let them reap the fruits of what they have sown.

Note: you cannot put a live person in the grave. So Sheol does

not refer to the grave it refers to living death as these betrayers experience the consequences of their actions.

Psalms 139:8

> *If I ascend into heaven, You are there; If I make my bed in hell, behold, You are there.*

Is this the grave? How can it be? The grave is where we place the mortal remains of a human being. The spirit and soul are no longer there. Our bodies never leave the earth. Our bodies are formed from the elements of the earth and when life leaves our bodies, the remains rot and decay in the grave and return to their original chemical and physical constituents.

You cannot hide in the grave because your spirit never goes to the grave, it returns to God's safekeeping. In his life, David had problems from time to time with personal sin. We know that sin separates us from God but David had a covenant with God so that even when he fell into the snare of sin and all the consequences thereof, God still knew where to find him. He didn't leave him or forsake him.

God knows the thoughts and intents of the hearts of all human beings. Whether in covenant with him or not, we cannot flee from his presence. He knows where we are and what we're doing and thinking every second of every day that we're alive on this earth.

Proverbs 5:5

> *Her feet go down to death, Her steps lay hold of hell. SHEOL*

Once again, Sheol is not the grave. Read the context below. These are real life, physical consequences that result from following the ways of the flesh, the world and the devil.

This is what has created the misery of our world. This is what causes all manner of pain, sickness, disease, disability, deformity, mental problems, poverty, violence, war and untimely death. This is Sheol and the instruction is to avoid the terrible destruction that results from poor choices that ignore the wisdom of God.

[1]My son, pay attention to my wisdom; Lend your ear to my understanding,

[2]That you may preserve discretion, And your lips may keep knowledge.

[3]For the lips of an immoral woman drip honey, And her mouth is smoother than oil;

[4]But in the end she is bitter as wormwood, Sharp as a two-edged sword.

[5]Her feet go down to death, Her steps lay hold of hell.

[6]Lest you ponder her path of life-- Her ways are unstable; You do not know them.

[7]Therefore hear me now, my children, And do not depart from the words of my mouth.

[8]Remove your way far from her, And do not go near the door of her house,

[9]Lest you give your honor to others, And your years to the cruel one;

[10]Lest aliens be filled with your wealth, And your labors go to the house of a foreigner;

[11]And you mourn at last, When your flesh and your body are consumed,

[12]And say: "How I have hated instruction, And my heart despised correction!

[13]I have not obeyed the voice of my teachers, Nor inclined my ear to those who instructed me!

Proverbs 7:27

Her house is the way to hell, Descending to the chambers of death.

Proverbs 7:27 from *Young's Literal Translation* reads:

The ways of Sheol -- her house, Going down unto inner chambers of death!

These are the ways of personal destruction that leads to terrible consequences or Living Death.

Proverbs 9

[13]A foolish woman is clamorous; She is simple, and knows nothing.

[14]For she sits at the door of her house, On a seat by the highest places of the city,

[15]To call to those who pass by, Who go straight on their way:

[16]"Whoever is simple, let him turn in here"; And as for him who lacks understanding, she says to him,

[17]"Stolen water is sweet, And bread eaten in secret is pleasant."

[18]But he does not know that the dead are there, That her guests are in the depths of hell (SHEOL).

Who is this foolish woman? In writing Proverbs, we know that Solomon wrote about wisdom as a beautiful, loving, faithful wife (Proverbs 31). But the opposite of wisdom is foolishness and he conveys the image of an adulterous, deceitful woman who seduces his people with her false illicit ways sending them down the path to personal and corporate destruction. She is a temptress and a liar and she represents the ways of the flesh, the world and the devil.

The dead follow her ways. Her guests dwell in misery and hopelessness. Not literally dead but dead in their spirit, devoid of understanding, subject to personal and corporate disaster. The depths of hell indicate just how ensnared they really are. Common examples include the stronghold of addiction, an incurable illness, major psychological problems or external, insurmountable difficulties. Eg: famine, prison, brutal enslavement.

Proverbs 15:11

Hell and Destruction are before the Lord; So how much more the hearts of the sons of men.

And from the *Revised Standard Version*:

Sheol and Abaddon lie open before the LORD, how much more the hearts of men!

We know what Sheol represents but what about this word **Abaddon**? As always, the bible will instruct us. In **Job:26v6**, we find a similar verse that says: Sheol is naked before him, and Destruction (Abaddon) has no covering.

We're talking about vulnerability. So **Abaddon** has no covering. This implies that at one point this mysterious entity did cover. Again the bible reveals all. In . . .

Ezekiel:28

14"*You were the anointed cherub who* **covers***; I established you; You were on the holy mountain of God; You walked back and forth in the midst of fiery stones.*
15*You were perfect in your ways from the day you were created, Till iniquity was found in you.*
16"*By the abundance of your trading You became filled with violence within, And you sinned; Therefore I cast you as a profane thing Out of the mountain of God; And I destroyed you, O* **covering** *cherub, From the midst of the fiery stones.*

This Anointed Cherub no longer **covers** (or protects) but is now synonymous with Destruction. So who is he? In . . .

Revelation 9:1

We read:

Then the fifth angel sounded: And I saw a star fallen from heaven to the earth. To him was given the key to the bottomless pit.

The star appears to be a reference to Satan when he was cast out of Heaven. He has influence over the inhabitants of the Earth but can only bring harm when authorised to do so by God as clearly shown in **Job**.

When judgement is decreed on the inhabitants of the Earth who bear the mark of the beast, there is to be a time of great destruction or "consequences".

Revelation 9 continues:

²And he opened the bottomless pit, and smoke arose out of the pit like the smoke of a great furnace. So the sun and the air were darkened because of the smoke of the pit.

³Then out of the smoke locusts came upon the earth. And to them was given power, as the scorpions of the earth have power.

⁴They were commanded not to harm the grass of the earth, or any green thing, or any tree, but only those men who do not have the seal of God on their foreheads.

⁵And they were not given authority to kill them, but to torment them for five months. Their torment was like the torment of a scorpion when it strikes a man.

⁶In those days men will seek death and will not find it; they will desire to die, and death will flee from them.

⁷The shape of the locusts was like horses prepared for battle. On their heads were crowns of something like gold, and their faces were like the faces of men.

⁸They had hair like women's hair, and their teeth were like lions' teeth.

⁹And they had breastplates like breastplates of iron, and the sound of their wings was like the sound of chariots with many horses running into battle.

¹⁰They had tails like scorpions, and there were stings in their tails. Their power was to hurt men five months.

¹¹And they had as king over them the angel of the bottomless pit, whose name in Hebrew is Abaddon, but in Greek he has the name Apollyon.

So **Abaddon** is the king of the bottomless pit and, in spite of assertions to the contrary, he is clearly identified as Satan.

So this verse from **Proverbs 15v11**: "Sheol and Abaddon lie open before the LORD, how much more the hearts of men!" refers to the way of Living Death (Sheol) and Satan (the One who deceives) as being clearly seen and understood by the Lord. He knows what's going on whereas most of us do not which is why we should listen to Him when He instructs us. If He knows what's going on with these powerful spiritual forces, He certainly knows what's going on in the hearts and minds of mortal men.

Proverbs 15:24

The way of life winds upward for the wise, That he may turn away from hell below.

A path of life [is] on high for the wise, To turn aside from Sheol beneath. (Young's Literal Translation)

The First and Great Commandment is to love the Lord your God with all your heart and acknowledge Him in all your ways. The quality of your life is governed by this. This verse confirms our absolute complete dependence upon Him.

Once we start ignoring Him, denying Him, resisting Him, we begin a steep downward trajectory that exposes us to greater temptation, greater sin and greater consequences.

Proverbs 23:14

You shall beat him with a rod, And deliver his soul from hell.

Thou with a rod smitest him, And his soul from Sheol thou deliverest. (Young's Literal Translation)

Not exactly politically correct in our "enlightened" Western society but the instruction, with promise, is very clear. Short, sharp, painful correction will produce a response that will cause the recipient to think twice before repeating the act that otherwise would lead him down the path to greater acts of wickedness. Causing harm both to himself and to others, which is the realm of Sheol.

I am reminded of a movie that I saw which was based on a true story about a young woman who was raised in a wealthy suburb in America. Her parents were "permissive and progressive enlightened individuals" who catered to her every whim. At age 16/17 she went to Australia on vacation and engaged in sexual relations with a boyfriend she met there. She had no clue about his past sexual history and was unaware that he was HIV positive. She contracted the AIDS virus from her very first sexual encounter. From that point on her life went down in a vicious cycle of self-destructive behaviour.

At one point in the movie she confronts her dad who is deeply distressed at his daughter's fate and she remonstrates with him saying, "Why didn't you ever discipline me? Why didn't you set the boundaries so I would know the difference between right and wrong? Now look at me, my life is ruined . . ."

What could her dad say to that? He listened to what the world was saying, instead of what God was saying and now his daughter was paying a terrible price for his naïvety.

Proverbs 27:20

Hell and Destruction are never full; So the eyes of man are never satisfied.

Sheol and Abaddon are never satisfied, Nor are the eyes of man ever satisfied. (New American Standard Bible)

This influence on mankind is what leads to his destruction. Without peace and contentment, Man is driven to greater acts of greed and selfish and dishonest gain. Sheol is his state of mind, Abaddon is his master. Only Jesus Christ can release him, person by person, from this tragic state.

Isaiah 14:9

"Hell from beneath is excited about you, To meet you at your coming; It stirs up the dead for you, All the chief ones of the earth; It has raised up from their thrones All the kings of the nations.

Sheol beneath hath been troubled at thee, To meet thy coming in, It is waking up *for thee Rephaim (demonic spirits), All chiefs ones of earth, It hath raised up from their thrones All kings of nations. (*Young's Literal Translation)

Make no mistake, this is out and out prophecy. It hasn't happened yet. The king of Babylon is yet another name assigned to Satan. He is the King, the Head, the Leader of Sheol. Revelation tells us that he is chained in a place of restraint for a period of 1,000 years after the judgement of the Earth has been fulfilled.

He will join his demons and they will marvel at his imposed restraint: (verse 10): "have you become as weak as we? Have you become like us?" **Isaiah 13** gives the full context.

With verses like this, it is easy to see how the current hell doctrine came to be formed. But it should still have been discarded and re-examined as soon as the Word of God began to look contradictory. This is why great care has to be taken before making assumptions.

Ezekiel 31:15

"Thus says the Lord God: 'In the day when it went down to hell, I caused mourning. I covered the deep because of it. I restrained its rivers, and the great waters were held back. I caused Lebanon to mourn for it, and all the trees of the field wilted because of it.

"Thus says the Lord GOD: When it goes down to Sheol I will make the deep mourn for it, and restrain its rivers, and many waters shall be stopped; I will clothe Lebanon in gloom for it, and all the trees of the field shall faint because of it. (Revised Standard Version)

Ezekiel 31:11

therefore I will deliver it into the hand of the mighty one of the nations, and he shall surely deal with it; I have driven it out for its wickedness.

Egypt is synonymous with sin. When judgement falls upon individual nations or, ultimately, upon the whole world. It is given over to Satan and his demons to wreak havoc on the inhabitants of the Earth.

Why? Because Man has chosen the ways of Sheol over the ways of God and if destruction is what he wants then destruction is what he will get. That is plagues, drought, infestation, brutality, war, starvation and death. The four horsemen of the Apocalypse. This is Sheol. This is hell. Not something beyond this life but the reality of our present lives. Could it be any clearer?

Ezekiel 31:16

I made the nations shake at the sound of its fall, when I cast it down to hell (Sheol) together with those who descend into the Pit; and all the trees of Eden, the choice and best of Lebanon, all that drink water, were comforted in the depths of the earth.

Demonic forces will be let loose and given free reign to bring about the madness and brutality of war. We've seen it happen through great deception before when the people of Germany were seduced into the Nazi desire for world domination. Ezekiel is a powerful prophetic warning for the world of today. We ignore it at our peril.

Ezekiel 31:17

They also went down to hell (Sheol) with it, with those slain by the sword; and those who were its strong arm dwelt in its shadows among the nations.

Everyone associated with the ways of this world will be dragged down into the same judgement. Nations that have made treaties where they have sold their virtues for a taste of this world's delicacies. Guilt by association, a fact as old as time itself. You fly with the crows, you get shot with them.

Ezekiel 32:21

The strong among the mighty Shall speak to him out of the midst of hell (Sheol)

With those who help him: 'They have gone down, They lie with the uncircumcised, slain by the sword.'

The uncircumcised are those who have given their allegiance to The Beast or the World's ways and systems. Who ignore the Sovereignty of God, who hate His ways. Who believe they are right in their own minds. The world looks up to men of great talent, intellect and physical prowess but they will witness them all being destroyed. The idolizing of individuals means nothing when we see just how powerless they are in the face of God's judgement.

Ezekiel 32:27

They do not lie with the mighty Who are fallen of the uncircumcised, Who have gone down to hell (Sheol) with their weapons of war; They have laid their swords under their heads, But their iniquities will be on their bones, Because of the terror of the mighty in the land of the living.

The oppressors seemed so strong, so invulnerable, but on the day of their judgement as they succumb to famine, to plague, to war, to pestilence, their terror is exposed for its weakness and uselessness in the face of judgement. This will all be witnessed by those who dwell upon the Earth and they will know that I am the Lord their God.

Daniel 12:2

*And many of those who sleep in **the dust of the earth** shall awake, Some to everlasting life, Some to shame and everlasting contempt.*

There is no mention of Sheol in this verse, yet it's used to justify current traditional teaching on hell. This verse is used to illustrate that there is only one resurrection where "the good" go to heaven and "the bad" go to hell. Read the verse again, it says no such thing.

Rather it confirms that everybody who dies, good or bad, is asleep until the time of their resurrection.

The First Resurrection is strictly for the righteous. The Second Resurrection is for everyone else who never received the Holy Spirit in this lifetime. There will be a Third Resurrection for those, in this life, that did receive the Holy Spirit and committed blasphemy against the Holy Spirit, for which there is no salvation:

Matthew 12:31

Therefore I say to you, every sin and blasphemy will be forgiven men, but the blasphemy against the Spirit will not be forgiven men.

Hebrews 10:29

Of how much worse punishment, do you suppose, will he be thought worthy who has trampled the Son of God underfoot, counted the blood of the covenant by which he was sanctified a common thing, and insulted the Spirit of grace?

That concludes with the final test and the "Gehenna" fire we will look at shortly, which destroys all those who were given the Holy Spirit, yet have made a deliberate, informed, conscious choice not to embrace God's ways but prefer the ways of the world.

Amos 9:2

Though they dig into hell (Sheol), From there my hand shall take them; Though they climb up to heaven, From there I will bring them down;

"Though they dig into hell" is not an allusion to hiding in a grave. It's a reference to looking to be saved from this trouble by relying on the world's system instead of turning to God. "Though they climb up to heaven" is not an allusion to hiding on a mountain or going up in a space ship, it's pursuing a righteous course based on their own strength. Without repentance and forgiveness there's no escape.

Habakkuk 2:5

Indeed, because he transgresses by wine, He is a proud man, And he does not stay at home. Because he enlarges his desire as hell, And he is like death, and cannot be satisfied, He gathers to himself all nations And heaps up for himself all peoples.

There is no contentment in pride. Here, hell (Sheol) is associated with never-ending excess and dissatisfaction.

Hell (Hades) in the New Testament

As we enter the New Testament, we change from the Hebrew language to the Greek language. We move from the priorities of the Old Covenant to the New Covenant.

The Old Covenant foreshadowed what was to be revealed in the New Covenant. We've seen that the law cannot be kept by weak human beings, so now we enter a new and better way of living where Jesus Christ, the Son of God, kept the law perfectly for us. He took our place for the punishment of all our sins and offers mercy and grace, instead of condemnation, to all believers who turn to Him and believe on His name and accept His sacrifice for their sins . . .

Under the Old Covenant, the Lord promised to bless the nation of Israel if they kept certain conditions that He laid down for them.

Under the New Covenant, it is still a 2-way street. There are certain things that believers need to do in order to remain under grace. If we deliberately sin or fail to do those things required of us, we end up back under the law and all its attendant consequences.

Please notice that these consequences (in the Greek language) are referred to as "Hades" which has exactly the same meaning as the Old Covenant word of Sheol.

There is one added dimension that did not exist under the Old Covenant. This is the prospect of the Second Death or Eternal

Punishment. In Greek, this word is Gehenna, or Eternal Fire.

As we will soon see, **this can only ever apply to believers who are found guilty of blasphemy against the Holy Spirit**. This is very serious but the warnings, related to that, only apply to a tiny number of scriptures. All the other warnings apply to the 2-way street principle that I have already explained.

So we will start with all the references as they relate to "Hades", which is the same as "Sheol".

But before we can do that, we will have to address the scriptures that refer to "outer darkness".

Outer Darkness

Matthew 8

> *[8]The centurion answered and said, "Lord, I am not worthy that you should come under my roof. But only speak a word, and my servant will be healed.*
> *[9]For I also am a man under authority, having soldiers under me. And I say to this one, 'go,' and he goes; and to another, 'come,' and he comes; and to my servant, 'do this,' and he does it."*
> *[10]When Jesus heard it, he marveled, and said to those who followed, "assuredly, I say to you, I have not found such great faith, not even in Israel!*
> *[11]And I say to you that many will come from east and west, and sit down with Abraham, Isaac, and Jacob in the kingdom of heaven. But the sons of the kingdom will be cast out into* **outer darkness**. *There will be weeping and gnashing of teeth."*

An allusion that the Jews would be cut off from the new dispensation of grace, exposing them to the consequences of the law because the old sacrifices have been superceded by the perfect sacrifice of Jesus Christ. From now on, there would be no access to grace but by Him.

Matthew 22:13

> *Then the king said to the servants, 'bind him hand and foot, take him away, and cast him into* **outer darkness***; there will be weeping and gnashing of teeth.'*

Failure to forgive others means our prayers will not be heard and we will not be forgiven which would bring us back under the law and all its consequences. Weeping means misery. Gnashing of teeth means frustration.

Matthew 25:30

> And cast the unprofitable servant into the **outer darkness**. There will be weeping and gnashing of teeth.'

Failure to grow in grace and knowledge, failure to demonstrate our faith in God's word by our actions, failure to fully participate in the great commission will render us unfruitful which would bring us back under the law and all its consequences.

Before we leave Matthew 25, we have to deal with the Sheep and Goats judgement because there is real potential for confusion.

In verse 32, we are told: "all the nations will be gathered before him, and he will separate them one from another, as a shepherd divides his sheep from the goats . . .

This is a clear reference to the Last Great Day Judgement as this is the only time when all the nations will be gathered before Him. (Psalm 86v9, Isaiah 66v18, Jeremiah 3v17, Micah 4v1-4) His plan must be to separate the nations so that they will exist within their own boundaries for the duration of the 100 year Judgement. This makes sense as all nations are predominantly families grown big. This is not a reference to punishing one nation over another.

But, this parable doesn't end there, or so it seems. As happens so often in the Bible, pieces are lumped together and made to look as if it is all one story. But anyone who studies prophecy quickly realises that one statement can contain allusions to 2 or 3 completely different events, just look at Daniel chapter 12, or any chapter in Revelation.

Not understanding this can lead any casual reader into all kinds of confusion because the next verse talks about something completely different:

In verse 33, he goes on to say: and He will set the sheep on his right hand, but the goats on the left.

He goes on to state the difference between those who served Him faithfully and those who didn't. This is not the separation of believers and unbelievers. This is talking about faithful Christians and unfaithful Christians.

These are Christians who never repented of their sins of omission (read the preceding story of the talents again). Instead of being led by the Holy Spirit and obeying his word, they did their own thing and His work suffered because of that. They ignored instruction and rebuke right up to the day of their death and blasphemed the Holy Spirit.

They sealed their fate which is announced in the final verse of this chapter.

As I said, it is critical that Bible scholars adhere with the greatest strictness to the instruction from the Bible not to allow private interpretation into any part of it.

Now we move onto those verses that contain the word "Hades". Hades is the Greek equivalent of the Hebrew word Sheol.

Hades in the New Testament

Matthew 11:23

*And you, Capernaum, who are exalted to heaven, will be brought down to **Hades**; for if the mighty works which were done in you had been done in Sodom, it would have remained until this day.*

Luke 10:15

*And you, Capernaum, who are exalted to heaven, will be brought down to **Hades**.*

Capernaum had received a powerful witness from the ministry of Jesus Christ. He did many miracles there but He was still ignored by many of the people. Jesus made the point that had He carried out those same works in the city of Sodom, the people would have repented and been delivered from the destruction they ultimately suffered. So Capernaum would now be judged and its people given over to the forces of darkness who would tempt them to their own destruction, in this lifetime, because they had rejected the works and teachings of Jesus and refused to repent.

Matthew 16:18

*And I also say to you that you are Peter, and on this rock I will build My church, and the gates of **Hades** shall not prevail against it.*

The world should be very careful how it treats the church of Jesus Christ. Modern-day followers are called Christians who are empowered intercessors who have access to The Father and have power and authority to intercede for those afflicted by the consequences of sin.

The flesh, the world and the devil are not permitted to harm those living under grace and they flee when confronted by two or more of them.

For a suffering unbeliever, who desires help in his time of need, he can do a lot worse than seek out the help of Christ's church.

THE BIG ONE (DANTÉ'S ERROR)

Luke 16:19-31

This is the big one. This is the parable that has convinced almost the entire Christian church of the Dante depiction of what some kind of eternal-hell-after-life must be like. This huge error in teaching could have been avoided had greater consideration been given to what Jesus was discussing just prior to delivering this parable.

In Luke, chapter 16, verse 19; Jesus begins telling a story about a rich man and a poor man called Lazarus. Please note, in no other parable, that Jesus told, did He actually give a name to one of the characters. This is highly significant as you will soon see . . .

> *19There was a certain rich man who was clothed in purple and fine linen and fared sumptuously every day.*

A big clue to what this is all about lies in the identity of the rich man. We know he was clothed in purple, which is synonymous with royalty. We also know he was clothed in fine linen which is synonymous with righteous acts and then there is the fact that he is rich and feasts every day. Biblically, this means he enjoys the best of everything: food, health, wisdom, relationships and protection. This is one prosperous individual in every sense of the word. He enjoys a "blessed" status in this life. So who is this rich man supposed to represent?

Well, if you read the preceding verses, you will discover that Jesus was talking to the Pharisees.

The Pharisees did not recognise or accept Jesus as being the Messiah (the Son of God). We also know, from preceding accounts, that Jesus had a habit of hiding deep spiritual meaning within these parables:

Matthew 13

> [10]*And the disciples came and said to Him, "Why do You speak to them in parables?"*
> [11]*He answered and said to them, "Because it has been given to YOU to know the mysteries of the Kingdom of heaven, but to them it has not been given.*

Remember, we still haven't discovered the identity of the rich man yet, so let's continue to examine the evidence.

Let's look at the 3 verses which immediately precede verse 19 of luke chapter 16 . . .

> [16]*The law and the prophets were until John. Since that time the kingdom of God has been preached, and everyone is pressing into it.*

This is massively significant. Jesus is announcing a cut-off of the entire Judeo model of living. John the baptist's life is concluding the entire Old Covenant. And in the same verse, Jesus has announced its replacement.

> [17]*And it is easier for heaven and earth to pass away than for one tittle of the law to fail.*

Now Jesus is confirming that every single requirement of the Old Covenant must be fulfilled, right down to the smallest comma or period and no one, up to that time, had been able to do it.

18Whoever divorces his wife and marries another commits adultery; and whoever marries her who is divorced from her husband commits adultery.

Has Jesus suddenly lost His train of thought? Why did He suddenly start talking about marriage?

Let's see . . .

Jesus is confirming that no marriage covenant could be dissolved by anything other than the death of one of the spouses. If a divorce has taken place, neither spouse, while they were alive, could re-marry without committing adultery.

Jesus was making a major point here. He is talking about a specific marriage. What is He referring to?

Isaiah 54

5For your Maker is your HUSBAND, The Lord of Hosts is His name; And your Redeemer is the Holy One of Israel; He is called the God of the whole earth.

Jeremiah 31

32not according to the covenant that I made with their fathers in the day that I took them by the hand to lead them out of the land of Egypt, My covenant which they broke, though I was a HUSBAND to them, says the Lord.

The marriage Jesus was referring to was the marriage he had with Israel under the auspices of the Old Covenant before He became God in the flesh. The Lord divorced Israel because of her unfaithful ways and her abandonment of Him.

But there was no way that God could initiate a New Marriage Covenant unless one of the parties died. So it was either going to have to be Jesus or every single living descendant of Abraham, Isaac, Jacob.

This New Marriage Covenant would be between Jesus Christ and the Church:

2 Corinthians 11

²*For I am jealous for you with godly jealousy. For I have betrothed you to one husband, that I may present you as a chaste virgin to Christ.*

And the Church is described as the Bride of Christ:

Revelation 21

⁹*Then one of the seven angels who had the seven bowls filled with the seven last plagues came to me and talked with me saying, "Come, I will show you the bride, the Lamb's wife."*

So now we know, the rich man was a reference to the Old Covenant and everyone who benefitted from the Old Covenant, namely the Jewish people, the observant descendants of the Nation of Israel and especially the priesthood.

So we've identified the rich man, what about the poor man? What do we know about Lazarus? Why did Jesus use this name for one of the characters in this parable? He never used names for His characters in previous parables. The bible reveals astonishing answers:

Luke 16

²⁰*But there was a certain beggar named Lazarus, full of sores, who was laid at his gate,*
²¹*desiring to be fed with the crumbs which fell from the rich man's table. Moreover the dogs came and licked his sores.*

Lazarus is described as a beggar. A beggar is not a profession it's a condition of life. His extreme poverty means that he is dependent on the charity of others. Typically, a beggar cannot do regular work because he is often afflicted with disablement or poor health. His relationships with family and friends is often estranged and many beggars live with constant physical pain, mental anguish and psychological problems. He is an outcast of society, despised, unwanted and ignored. His condition is hopeless. He is the living embodiment of someone living in a state of Sheol/Hades.

Lazarus is the complete anti-thesis of the rich man.

OK, so why give this beggar a name? Why did Jesus use the name Lazarus?

Well, earlier in His ministry, Jesus came across a man called Lazarus and this account is recorded in: **John 11 v1-45**.

There is more prophetic significance in this chapter than most biblical scholars have realised.

This chapter concentrates on how Jesus raised Lazarus from the dead. Some scholars insist that this was representative of Jesus being raised from the dead, but the scriptures don't support that theory.

First of all, Lazarus had been dead for at least four days, not three:

John 11

   [17]So when Jesus came, He found that he had already been in the tomb four days.

Remember, we're trying to identify who Lazarus is supposed to represent; so who else has been dead for at least four days? Well, in **2 Peter 3v8**, we are told that "a day to God is as a thousand years". So who has been dead for four thousand years without hope, without help? Isn't it the gentiles, all those nations other than Israel? Is this who Lazarus is supposed to represent, the gentiles? Let's keep gathering the evidence . . .

Jesus was in the grave for 3 days, not 4. This is crucial because Jesus said there would only be one sign that this generation would be given as to who He really was which was the sign of what happened to Jonah: (**Matthew 12v40, Matthew 16v4** and **Luke 11v29**) that's 2-3 witnesses within scripture that this was the case, unlike Lazarus who is never mentioned in that connection.

Jesus was first notified of Lazarus' condition when he was just sick, He could easily have healed Lazarus, but He allowed him to die, why? So Jesus could demonstrate the truth of the Resurrection of the Dead to His disciples and the rest of us: (**John 11 v15 & v24**).

This is extraordinarily important for you to understand: Lazarus was not resurrected to Eternal Life with an incorruptible body. He was resurrected back to PHYSICAL LIFE. Martha, in **verse 24**, spoke of the Judgement of the Last Great Day, which she spoke of in hope concerning her brother.

In **verses 33, 34 & 35**, Jesus is deeply grieved. Jesus wept, not just because of Mary's grief, but the grief of all humankind that have mourned the passing of a loved one. This was empathy on a scale that you and I can't possibly imagine.

This is what took Jesus to the cross, this was the love that held Him there. We have so corrupted the gospel of the kingdom of God and failed to tell the whole truth of what Jesus did. No wonder this parable about Lazarus and the rich man has been so distorted and corrupted. It's too revealing and its message is glorious . . .

You see, the beggar is the New Covenant delivered to the gentiles, the non-Israelites, the ones who were shut out by the Old Covenant. The ones who, when they suffered, could only be comforted by the dogs (the unclean ones). The name given by Jews to the gentiles: (*see* **Matthew 15v26 & Mark 7v27**).

Okay, now that we've established the identity of the two main characters, we can now move through the rest of the parable which is jaw-droppingly awesome . . .

Luke 16

²²*So it was that the beggar died,*

The gentiles, who repent, die in the baptism of water and are immediately resurrected to a new and better life in Christ . . .. IN THIS LIFE! Note: there is no mention of burial, because Jesus rose from the dead, the grave couldn't hold him . . .

²²*and was carried by the angels to Abraham's bosom.*

Remember the promises given by God to Abraham after he nearly sacrificed his son Isaac? The Lord said because you have not withheld your son, all, all, all the Nations of the Earth shall be blessed through your Seed. The physical lineage of Jesus Christ, on his mother's side, originated from Abraham, *see* Genesis 2v18.

²²*The rich man also died and was buried.*

The rich man (the Old Covenant) also died. The implication is that they both died at the same time. The Old Covenant died with Jesus. He founded it, He ended it and He buried it, there would be no resurrection of the Old Covenant.

²³*And being in torments in Hades,*

There was no more forgiveness of sins in the rituals of the Old Covenant. Jesus Christ kept the whole law. He fulfilled everything in His life, His death and His resurrection. The Old Covenant rituals were a foreshadow of things to come. Well now Jesus was here. Everything was fulfilled in Him. So anyone who finds themselves in a state of torment and hopelessness must now come to Christ for deliverance. All the followers of the Old Covenant that still try to rely on rituals and animal sacrifices are wasting their time. They will continue in their sins and the consequences of those sins until they recognise that everything has changed. No one can escape the law or receive mercy against its consequences except through Jesus. Without Jesus, we all live in Hades, a state of hopelessness, a state of living death, a state of Hell. So this rich man is now in a state of torment. The original source of his rich life has gone . . .

²³*he lifted up his eyes and saw Abraham afar off, and Lazarus in his bosom.*

Those still clinging to the Old Covenant cannot understand why the old ways are not enough any more. They look at the Christian Church with all their blessings that used to belong to them, but now it seems they are enduring all the hardships of life and they see the promises of Abraham enshrined in Christian belief, experience and teaching.

²⁴*Then he cried and said, 'Father Abraham, have mercy on me, and send Lazarus that he may dip the tip of his finger in water and cool my tongue; for I am tormented in this flame.'*

The old sacrifices no longer apply. The old sacrificial system has been superceded by the perfect sacrifice of Jesus Christ. To get relief from trouble, the only way to mercy, forgiveness and deliverance is now through Jesus Christ alone.

²⁵*But Abraham said, 'Son,* [talking to Israel] *remember that in your lifetime* [during the course of time when the Old Covenant existed] *you received your good things,* [all the physical blessings of the Old Covenant] *and likewise Lazarus evil things;* [The Gentiles had no hope, no knowledge and no covenant with God and therefore were always suffering from the consequences of the Law and their lack of enlightenment] *but now he is*

comforted [by the New Covenant] *and you are tormented.* [Because you have rejected the Messiah and the New Covenant in His blood].

²⁶*And besides all this, between us and you there is a great gulf fixed,* [No one can come to the Father unless the Spirit of God draw him and no one has access to the Father except through Jesus Christ].

so that those who want to pass from here to you cannot, nor can those from there pass to us.' [You don't put new wine into old wine skins. You cannot mix oil and water. The Old Covenant testified of Jesus Christ. The New Covenant is in Jesus Christ. The Old Covenant was based on ritual and animal sacrifices. The New Covenant is based on faith and relationship].

²⁷*Then he said, 'I beg you therefore, father, that you would send him to my father's house,*

A clear reference to the Jewish temple.

²⁸*for I have five brothers, that he may testify to them,*

Annas was the chief high priest at this time and had five sons and a son-in-law called Caiaphas, who all, as it turns out, played a part in the trial of Jesus. (*source*: Josephus)

lest they also come to this place of torment.'

Remember, this place of torment used to be their hope of deliverance. Their adherence to Old Covenant practices, especially the sacrificial laws, was what brought them redemption. That relationship with God died when the Husband of that relationship died. So God is no longer bound to honour that agreement. That covenant has been superceded by the New Covenant.

²⁹*Abraham said to him, 'They have Moses and the prophets; let them hear them.'*

Moses and the prophets testified of this new and better Covenant, its new and better promises . . .

> [30] *And he said, 'No, father Abraham; but if one goes to them from the dead, they will repent.'*
> [31] *But he said to him, 'If they do not hear Moses and the prophets, neither will they be persuaded though one rise from the dead.'*

Jesus' miracles were not enough. Remember how they reacted to Lazarus rising from the dead? The transformation of someone's way of thinking has to originate from the calling of God and the recipient's willing response. The calling itself is an act of mercy.

It is so regrettable that for generations the Christian Church has forced an interpretation onto this parable that has led to misunderstanding and confusion. It was never intended to be used as a support for a doctrine that consigned all unbelievers to an eternal existence of conscious suffering.

This doctrinal error has caused much anguish, fear and despair and grossly misrepresented the teaching of the kingdom of God.

Now let us continue our look at what Hades (Sheol) truly represents . . .

Acts 2:27

> *For You will not leave my soul in Hades, Nor will You allow Your Holy One to see corruption.*

Acts 2:31

> *he, foreseeing this, spoke concerning the resurrection of the Christ, that His soul was not left in Hades, nor did His flesh see corruption.*

In this context, speaking of Christ, most commentators assume that Peter was speaking of Hades as the grave. So why not use the word grave? Because, as with Sheol, Hades is more accurately defined as a state of hopelessness, the way of death and misery, the way of life for most people. The way of this world.

The soul does not go to the grave. It's the body that goes into the ground, the soul and the spirit return to God.

There is another assumption that because Jesus became sin for us, He was sent to some underground place where all the other "souls" are kept in some form of suspended animation pending judgement.

Believe that and you would end up tearing up nearly two-thirds of the rest of the bible.

These verses simply say that Jesus was not to be left in this world and that His flesh would never be corrupted by this world. He overcame this world. He overcame the weakness of the flesh.

Let us never use human reasoning to determine what the bible is saying.

1 Corinthians 15:55

> "O Death, where is your sting? O Hades, where is your victory?"

Death, without the hope of resurrection; that's death with a sting. Hades, or the way of death, has no victory once an individual has been delivered through grace either in this life or the next.

Revelation 1:18

> I am He who lives, and was dead, and behold, I am alive forevermore. Amen. And I have the keys of Hades and of Death.

Once again, Jesus is speaking and He makes a clear delineation between death and Hades. He defeated actual physical death (the cessation of conscious existence) by physical resurrection and He defeated the way of death: that separation between God and man that leads to all kinds of misery.

He holds the keys to both because He defeated both and Christians know this better than anyone because we receive the fruits of that blessing every day of our lives.

Revelation 6:8

> So I looked, and behold, a pale horse. And the name of him who sat on it was Death, and Hades followed with him. And power was given to them over a fourth of the earth, to kill with sword, with hunger, with death, and by the beasts of the earth.

Consistently, throughout the history of man, one-fourth of the human population, alive at any one time, has suffered premature death by violence, famine and pestilence.

Note that the scripture says: "Hades followed death". It doesn't say Hades preceded death which, according to all other scriptures, it should do. So is this an error?

No it isn't. As with the Hebrew word Sheol, Hades is a contextual word that changes in meaning depending on its use.

For example, let me take a simple English word like field:

I could say that a dog ran around in a green field and everyone would know that I'm referring to a meadow or a park.

Or, I could say that a professor was highly knowledgeable in the field of physics and everyone would know that I'm referring to an area of expertise.

Same word, same spelling but contextually very different.

So, in this verse, "Hades follows death" means that death was followed by a sense of complete despair and mourning as there was no knowledge or hope of resurrection, only the pain of loss for those left behind. Not some eternal hellfire damnation . . .

Revelation 20:13

> The sea gave up the dead who were in it, and Death and Hades delivered up the dead who were in them. And they were judged, each one according to his works.

I sometimes get the impression that Jesus is teasing us a little bit here. Anyone reading this verse is going to be left scratching their head.

We know the last part of the verse is dealing with the Great White Throne Judgement (the Last Great Day) when all the unsaved dead will be resurrected back to a Second Physical Life.

But the first part doesn't make sense. Why distinguish drowning victims from anyone else? And if this refers to drowning victims, why say "The Sea", why not say the seas or the waters?

Because "The Sea" is a reference to the Global Dead. I'll leave it to others to explain but a study on this begins with the Temple of Solomon which is where "The Sea" is first fully described.

Now the middle bit. This reference to "death" only applies to human beings that died in their sins, but Hades isn't. So why use that term?

When a human being dies, he escapes from Hades (life in this world). Hades is not a holding place for the dead, or is it?

Besides human beings, who else has been held captive by the curse of separation from God? I refer you to an intriguing scripture found in

1 Corinthians 6v3 where Paul states that the church will judge angels, fallen angels. These demons (rebels) possess and influence rebellious human beings and help bring about many of the calamities of this life and the Church can and will be judging them. (**Colossians 1v20**).

You see, demons don't die. (**Isaiah 24 v21,22; 2 Peter 2v4; Jude 1v6**) They're trapped in Hades (in their state of hopelessness). They're the only ones that this part of the verse can be referring to. Human beings have to be physically alive in order to be in Hades. So the "dead" that inhabit Hades are those who can't escape from it.

Remember, Jesus Christ created them as well.

Revelation 20:14

> *Then Death and Hades were cast into the lake of fire. This is the second death.*

> *Death and She'ol were thrown into the lake of fire. This is the second death (GEHENNA), the lake of fire. (Hebrew Names Version)*

No more death, no more crying, no more pain, no more sorrow. The Second Death is permanent, to be made as if they had never existed. Unrepentant men, women and angels who knowingly rejected everything God had offered them will cease to exist, burned up in an explosion of fire that will devour the entire surface of the earth.

Eternal suffering? No. Eternal death? Yes . . .

So, at the end of one hundred years (the Last Great Day), after the Final Test, the whole planet will be burned up with Gehenna fire and death will die with the Earth and all the ways of death which have tormented mankind throughout his generations will die with it and take with them all those who still held a desire for the former ways and therefore succumbed to the final temptation. Eternal life was not their aspiration so they shall be made as if they had never been.

Gehenna

A SERIOUS SOBER WARNING TO CHRISTIANS

This concludes all biblical references to Sheol and Hades, their context and biblical explanation. But this still leaves us with "Gehenna".

There's no getting away from it, this is a very serious Judgement that is both Final and Permanent and must be avoided at all costs.

It should be noted that Gehenna is not mentioned until the New Testament. We further note that it's used in conjunction with the term: "Second Death". So this obviously does not apply to ordinary people living in THIS life, it certainly doesn't apply to unbelievers because they're being judged and evaluated under the Law and their lives are affected by the consequences of either keeping or breaking those laws. So who is it aimed at?

Well it can only apply to those who are already living their Second Life.

The bible is entirely consistent. Believers are described as individuals who have been Born Again, but that can't happen unless they die first. Symbolically, this is what happens with water baptism. The sinner is completely immersed into a watery grave and when he/she emerges, they're being resurrected into a new life (a Second Life) and the Holy Spirit is conferred upon him/her by the laying on of hands by Elders of the Church.

From that point on, the sinner lives in a cleansed state. All his sins forgiven (promise) so long as he/she maintains his/her part in the new covenant (condition).

Some choose to argue these points in the Grace versus Works debate. There is ample teaching that covers this so I'm not going to re-play it in this book. I would only point out that the Old Covenant was based on obedience to the law and sacrificial rituals. The New Covenant is based on the instructions of Jesus Christ and faith which leads to fruitful works of righteousness (please read the entire book of James).

So, for Christians, we are living in our "Second Life" already. When our physical life is over, we don't get resurrected back to a Second Physical Life, we go straight into an Eternal existence . . . Or not!

Yes, that's right. **It's the greatest deceit of all time, to convince the Church to preach to unbelievers that they will be eternally damned if they don't convert to Christianity. When the warning of eternal judgement is not directed at unbelievers, but at unfaithful Christians.**

As we're about to see, the Gehenna judgement can only apply to unfaithful Christians, not to anyone else.

This is all about the Holy Spirit. So let's start with some contrasts shall we. What can this world offer us in exchange for the Holy Spirit? How about a gigantic lottery win? How about being made king or President? How about an unbelievably gorgeous wife or an absolute Adonis of a husband?

Money, power, sex, what would you trade the Holy Spirit for?

Don't be so quick to answer. The fact is, in the Church today, the Holy Spirit is being traded off for other priorities that are worth considerably less than what I've just suggested. The compromises and trade-offs are considerable. For a start, there are hangovers from our old (first) life that we are unwilling to abandon:

WE MUST CUT OFF OUR BODY PARTS?

Matthew 5:29

If your right eye causes you to sin, pluck it out and cast it from you; for it is more profitable for you that one of your members perish, than for your whole body to be cast into hell. (Gehenna)

Matthew 5:30

And if your right hand causes you to sin, cut it off and cast it from you; for it is more profitable for you that one of your members perish, than for your whole body to be cast into hell. (Gehenna)

Matthew 18

[8]And if your hand or foot causes you to sin, cut it off and cast it from you. It is better for you to enter into life lame or maimed, rather than having two hands or two feet, to be cast into the everlasting fire.
[9]And if your eye causes you to sin, pluck it out and cast it from you. It is better for you to enter into life with one eye, rather than having two eyes, to be cast into hell fire. (Gehenna)

Mark 9:43

If your hand causes you to sin, cut it off. It is better for you to enter into life maimed, rather than having two hands, to go to hell (Gehenna), into the fire that shall never be quenched

Mark 9:45

And if your foot causes you to sin, cut it off. It is better for you to enter life lame, rather than having two feet, to be cast into hell (Gehenna), into the fire that shall never be quenched

Mark 9:47

> *And if your eye causes you to sin, pluck it out. It is better for you to enter the kingdom of God with one eye, rather than having two eyes, to be cast into hell (Gehenna) fire-*

Seven times. Seven times? This point is so crucial that it's highlighted seven times? According to Jesus, what He is referring to is so serious, it will have eternal consequences for the offender. So we dare not speculate as to what He's referring to, so we need scripture to interpret scripture.

Notice that Jesus specifies three distinct parts of the human body:

The right eye x 2,

The right hand x 3,

And one foot x 2.

Why not specify a nose, a leg or an arm? No, Jesus was being specific for a reason . . .

The context of **Matthew 5** are the promises and conditions of the New Covenant that are expanded upon throughout the rest of the New Testament.

The context of **Matthew 18** is the emphasis of humility in Christian living.

The context of **Mark 9** is service.

The EYE sees,

The HAND does,

The FOOT goes.

So we've got influence, attitude, work and obedience that affects the life of a believer. A believer starts his Second Life as a New Creation. He has been cleansed from all his sins and, get this, God comes to live in him and that person is made Holy. But, but, but, he does not lose the right to self determination. He can freely choose to keep on sinning. He can freely choose not to learn the new disciplines that will help him make wise decisions. He can freely choose worldly, fleshly influences over the influence of the Holy Spirit.

Human nature tempts and compels us toward sin and selfishness. The divine nature leads, directs and empowers us toward righteousness and is the source of Godly love.

The Christian makes a daily choice to have Christ at the centre of his life . . . Or . . . he can go and do his own thing.

Such a decision grieves the Holy Spirit and exposes the Christian to corrupt influences. This pulls him further and further away and, if not corrected in this lifetime, leaves him eternally condemned.

Hebrews 6

> [4]For it is impossible for those who were once enlightened, and have tasted the heavenly gift, and have become partakers of the Holy Spirit,
> [5]and have tasted the good word of God and the powers of the age to come,
> [6]if they fall away, to renew them again to repentance, since they crucify again for themselves the Son of God, and put Him to an open shame.
> [7]For the earth which drinks in the rain that often comes upon it, and bears herbs useful for those by whom it is cultivated, receives blessing from God;
> [8]but if it bears thorns and briars, it is rejected and near to being cursed, whose end is to be burned.

Can a murderer go back to being a murderer? Can a liar go back to being a liar? Can an adulterer go back to committing adultery? That isn't evidence of a new life and it certainly isn't the fruit of the Holy Spirit.

Our eyes are opened so we should seek discernment of things revealed by the Spirit through the Word of God. If our eyes are still drawn to worldly views that contradict this new insight then we must pluck it out and get rid of it, no matter what the initial cost to us may be.

The right hand symbolises the work we do. If our job grieves our conscience or interferes unduly with our new life, we should cut it off and seek the work God has set aside for us. This includes our part in the Great Commission. We earn money from our work, do we invest it in worldly institutions? Or do we invest it into the Kingdom of God?

Matthew 25

> [41]*Then He will also say to those on the left hand, 'Depart from Me, you cursed, into the everlasting fire prepared for the devil and his angels:*
> [42]*for I was hungry and you gave Me no food; I was thirsty and you gave Me no drink;*
> [43]*I was a stranger and you did not take Me in, naked and you did not clothe Me, sick and in prison and you did not visit Me.'*
> [44]*Then they also will answer Him, saying, 'Lord, when did we see You hungry or thirsty or a stranger or naked or sick or in prison, and did not minister to You?'*
> [45]*Then He will answer them, saying, 'Assuredly, I say to you, inasmuch as you did not do it to one of the least of these, you did not do it to Me.'*
> [46]*And these will go away into everlasting punishment, but the righteous into eternal life."*

There are many Christian ministries that are desperately under-resourced because of the lack of support that should be coming from Christians who are blessed with substantial physical resources.

They have these resources tied up in worldly institutions. Such men and women really need to re-think their priorities.

And lastly there are the feet. What direction are we going in?

Hebrews 12

> [6]*For whom the Lord loves He chastens, And scourges every son whom He receives."*
>
> [7]*If you endure chastening, God deals with you as with sons; for what son is there whom a father does not chasten?*
>
> [8]*But if you are without chastening, of which all have become partakers, then you are illegitimate and not sons.*
>
> [9]*Furthermore, we have had human fathers who corrected us, and we paid them respect. Shall we not much more readily be in subjection to the Father of spirits and live?*
>
> [10]*For they indeed for a few days chastened us as seemed best to them, but He for our profit, that we may be partakers of His holiness*
>
> [11]*Now no chastening seems to be joyful for the present, but painful; nevertheless, afterward it yields the peaceable fruit of righteousness to those who have been trained by it.*
>
> [12]*Therefore strengthen the hands which hang down, and the feeble knees,*
>
> [13]*and* **make straight paths for your feet**, *so that what is lame may not be dislocated, but rather be healed.*
>
> [14]*Pursue peace with all people, and holiness, without which no one will see the Lord:*
>
> [15]*looking carefully lest anyone fall short of the grace of God; lest any root of bitterness springing up cause trouble, and by this many become defiled;*
>
> [16]*lest there be any fornicator or profane person like Esau, who for one morsel of food sold his birthright.*
>
> [17]*For you know that afterward, when he wanted to inherit the blessing, he was rejected, for he found no place for repentance, though he sought it diligently with tears.*

Every Christian has to work out his salvation with fear and trembling **(Phillippians 2v12-16)**. Even Paul was aware that he could lose his salvation (**1 Corinthians 9v27**). Many teachers point out assurances in scripture that our salvation is assured. Well, from God's perspective, it is. No man can rob you of it. But, but, but, **you** can!

You make the decisions about your life. How much time you spend in prayer, study and fellowship is down to you. How you behave and treat others in the Church and in this world is down to you. How much time, effort and money you commit to "The Great Commission" is down to you.

Please read more on this in my book . . . *Miraculous Healing for the Church*.

Where else do we find warnings about Gehenna?

Matthew 5:22

But I say to you that whoever is angry with his brother without a cause shall be in danger of the judgment. And whoever says to his brother, 'Raca!' shall be in danger of the council. But whoever says, 'You fool!' shall be in danger of hell fire (Gehenna).

Remember where Jesus said, "a New Commandment I give to you to love one another"?

That's not advice, that's a command.

There are hundreds, if not thousands, of scriptures in the New Testament that cover this. Suffice to say, if you have a problem with a brother/sister in the Church, you would be safer sitting in a bath of acid, than not dealing with it. **Treat it as a matter of life and death, because it is**. It's the number one cause of sickness in the Body of Christ today, across all denominations . . .

By the way, loving your brother does not mean letting him wallow in ignorance. If he needs to be confronted then do it . . Christ's way.

James 5

> [19]*Brethren, if anyone among you wanders from the truth, and someone turns him back,*
>
> [20]*let him know that he who turns a sinner from the error of his way will save a soul from death and cover a multitude of sins.*

Another problem for modern-day religious teachers is fear of death. No one can effectively serve Christ in ministry if they are concerned about preserving their physical life. If fear of death is a concern for anyone in ministry; they will compromise their message to save their life. That means they have not been properly prepared for service and should step back, because they're a threat to the gospel and The Great Commission:

Matthew 10:28

> *And do not fear those who kill the body but cannot kill the soul. But rather fear Him who is able to destroy both soul and body in hell (Gehenna).*

Luke 12:5

> *But I will show you whom you should fear: Fear Him who, after He has killed, has power to cast into hell (Gehenna); yes, I say to you, fear Him!*

Those who teach are subject to a stricter judgement than those who don't. Also teachers are not permitted to teach those things that they are not already practicing themselves. There is only one outcome for hypocrites . . .

Matthew 23:15

> *Woe to you, scribes and Pharisees, hypocrites! For you travel land and sea to win one proselyte, and when he is won, you make him twice as much a son of hell (Gehenna) as yourselves.*

Matthew 23:33

Serpents, brood of vipers! How can you escape the condemnation of hell (Gehenna)?

James 3:6

And the tongue is a fire, a world of iniquity. The tongue is so set among our members that it defiles the whole body, and sets on fire the course of nature; and it is set on fire by hell (Gehenna).

All violence starts with the tongue. **Christians have a lifetime to master what they say and how they say it.** Everything we say is being recorded and what we say can and will have eternal consequences. **There is no question that warnings about Gehenna only apply to Christians.** But we have nothing to worry about so long as we keep Jesus Christ at the centre of our lives and He will see us safely through. I must urge all my Christian readers to get a copy of *Miraculous Healing for the Church,* as it goes into much greater detail about the current responsibilities of individual Christians and churches that will highlight the scriptures you most need to know.

We conclude this major study on hell by looking at the only scripture in the bible that has the word *tartarus* as a description of hell:

2 Peter 2:4

For if God did not spare the angels who sinned, but cast them down to hell (Tartarus) and delivered them into chains of darkness, to be reserved for judgment;

This one is easy-peasy. It's simply a reference to:

Revelation 20

¹Then I saw an angel coming down from heaven, having the key to the bottomless pit and a great chain in his hand.

²He laid hold of the dragon, that serpent of old, who is the Devil and Satan, and bound him for a thousand years;

³and he cast him into the bottomless pit [Tartarus], and shut him up, and set a seal on him, so that he should deceive the nations no more till the thousand years were finished. But after these things he must be released for a little while.

This final set of scriptures on Gehenna I left until last because it summarises the condition of those who are in the greatest danger of the Second Death:

Jude

⁴For certain men have crept in unnoticed, who long ago were marked out for this condemnation, ungodly men, who turn the grace of our God into lewdness and deny the only Lord God and our Lord Jesus Christ.

⁵But I want to remind you, though you once knew this, that the Lord, having saved the people out of the land of Egypt, afterward destroyed those who did not believe.

⁶And the angels who did not keep their proper domain, but left their own abode, He has reserved in everlasting chains under darkness for the judgment of the great day; (Tartarus)

⁷as Sodom and Gomorrah, and the cities around them in a similar manner to these, having given themselves over to sexual immorality and gone after strange flesh, are set forth as an example, suffering the vengeance of eternal fire.

⁸Likewise also these dreamers defile the flesh, reject authority, and speak evil of dignitaries.

¹²These are spots in your love feasts, while they feast with you without fear, serving only themselves. They are clouds without water, carried about by the winds; late autumn trees without fruit, twice dead (Gehenna), pulled up by the roots;

¹³raging waves of the sea, foaming up their own shame; wandering stars for whom is reserved the blackness of darkness forever.

Christians must exercise extreme caution when listening, seeing or reading anything that purports to be Christian truth, including this book. You should only follow the teachings of the Bible and put your faith and trust in the scriptures. Remember, no authors, pastors or priests have died for you, only Christ. So listen to him, do what He says and you'll stay on safe ground.

Grave Scriptures

The study of hell would be incomplete without looking at all the scriptures that refer to the grave, commentary is reserved for "grave" scriptures that don't have an obvious reference to physical interment . . .

Genesis 35:20

And Jacob set a pillar on her grave, which is the pillar of Rachel's grave to this day.

Genesis 37:35

And all his sons and all his daughters arose to comfort him; but he refused to be comforted, and he said, "For I shall go down into the grave to my son in mourning." Thus his father wept for him.

Genesis 42:38

But he said, "My son shall not go down with you, for his brother is dead, and he is left alone. If any calamity should befall him along the way in which you go, then you would bring down my gray hair with sorrow to the grave."

Genesis 44:29

But if you take this one also from me, and calamity befalls him, you shall bring down my gray hair with sorrow to the grave.'

Genesis 44:31

it will happen, when he sees that the lad is not with us, that he will die. So your servants will bring down the gray hair of your servant our father with sorrow to the grave.

Genesis 50:5

'My father made me swear, saying, "Behold, I am dying; in my grave which I dug for myself in the land of Canaan, there you shall bury me." Now therefore, please let me go up and bury my father, and I will come back.' "

Numbers 19:16

Whoever in the open field touches one who is slain by a sword or who has died, or a bone of a man, or a grave, shall be unclean seven days.

Numbers 19:18

A clean person shall take hyssop and dip it in the water, sprinkle it on the tent, on all the vessels, on the persons who were there, or on the one who touched a bone, the slain, the dead, or a grave.

Deuteronomy 34:6

And He buried him in a valley in the land of Moab, opposite Beth Peor; but no one knows his grave to this day.

1 Samuel 2:6

"The Lord kills and makes alive; He brings down to the grave and brings up.

2 Samuel 3:32

So they buried Abner in Hebron; and the king lifted up his voice and wept at the grave of Abner, and all the people wept.

2 Samuel 19:37

Please let your servant turn back again, that I may die in my own city, near the grave of my father and mother. But here is your servant Chimham; let him cross over with my lord the king, and do for him what seems good to you."

1 Kings 2:6

Therefore do according to your wisdom, and do not let his gray hair go down to the grave in peace.

1 Kings 2:9

Now therefore, do not hold him guiltless, for you are a wise man and know what you ought to do to him; but bring his gray hair down to the grave with blood."

1 Kings 14:13

And all Israel shall mourn for him and bury him, for he is the only one of Jeroboam who shall come to the grave, because in him there is found something good toward the Lord God of Israel in the house of Jeroboam.

2 Kings 22:20

Surely, therefore, I will gather you to your fathers, and you shall be gathered to your grave in peace; and your eyes shall not see all the calamity which I will bring on this place." ' " So they brought back word to the king.

2 Chronicles 34:28

Surely I will gather you to your fathers, and you shall be gathered to your grave in peace; and your eyes shall not see all the calamity which I will bring on this place and its inhabitants." ' " So they brought back word to the king.

Job 3:22

Who rejoice exceedingly, And are glad when they can find the grave?

Job 5:26

You shall come to the grave at a full age, As a sheaf of grain ripens in its season.

Job 7:9 NKJ

As the cloud disappears and vanishes away, So he who goes down to the grave does not come up.

Job 10:19

I would have been as though I had not been. I would have been carried from the womb to the grave.

Job 14:13

"Oh, that You would hide me in the grave, That You would conceal me until Your wrath is past, That You would appoint me a set time, and remember me!

Job 17:1

"My spirit is broken, My days are extinguished, The grave is ready for me.

Job 17:13

If I wait for the grave as my house, If I make my bed in the darkness,

Job 21:13

They spend their days in wealth, And in a moment go down to the grave.

Job 21:32

Yet he shall be brought to the grave, And a vigil kept over the tomb.

Job 24:19

As drought and heat consume the snow waters, So the grave consumes those who have sinned.

This scripture is about spiritual death (Sheol), not literal death as in a physical grave.

Psalms 6:5

For in death there is no remembrance of You; In the grave who will give You thanks?

Psalms 30:3

O Lord, You brought my soul up from the grave; You have kept me alive, that I should not go down to the pit.

The soul doesn't go to the physical grave, this is a reference to Sheol as David experienced momentary separation.

Psalms 31:17

Do not let me be ashamed, O Lord, for I have called upon You; Let the wicked be ashamed; Let them be silent in the grave.

Psalms 49:14

Like sheep they are laid in the grave; Death shall feed on them; The upright shall have dominion over them in the morning; And their beauty shall be consumed in the grave, far from their dwelling.

Psalms 49:15

But God will redeem my soul from the power of the grave, For He shall receive me. Selah

Psalms 88:3

For my soul is full of troubles, And my life draws near to the grave.

Psalms 88:5

Adrift among the dead, Like the slain who lie in the grave, Whom You remember no more, And who are cut off from Your hand.

Psalms 88:11

Shall Your lovingkindness be declared in the grave? Or Your faithfulness in the place of destruction?

Psalms 89:48

What man can live and not see death? Can he deliver his life from the power of the grave? Selah

Psalms 141:7

Our bones are scattered at the mouth of the grave, As when one plows and breaks up the earth.

Proverbs 30:16

The grave, The barren womb, The earth that is not satisfied with water-- And the *fire never says, "Enough!"*

Death constantly consumes.

Ecclesiastes 9:10

Whatever your hand finds to do, do it with your might; for there is no work or device or knowledge or wisdom in the grave where you are going.

Exactly. Physical death has no conscious existence until resurrection.

Song of Solomon 8:6

The Shulamite to Her Beloved Set me as a seal upon your heart, As a seal upon your arm; For love is as strong as death, Jealousy as cruel as the grave; Its flames are flames of fire, A most vehement flame.

Passion is as deep an emotion as grief.

Isaiah 14:19

But you are cast out of your grave Like an abominable branch, Like the garment of those who are slain, Thrust through with a sword, Who go down to the stones of the pit, Like a corpse trodden underfoot.

Isaiah 53:9

And they made His grave with the wicked-- But with the rich at His death, Because He had done no violence, Nor was any deceit in His mouth.

A prophecy about Jesus in the tomb

Jeremiah 20:17

Because he did not kill me from the womb, That my mother might have been my grave, And her womb always enlarged with me.

Ezekiel 32:23

Her graves are set in the recesses of the Pit, And her company is all around her *grave, **All of them slain, fallen by the sword**, Who caused terror in the land of the living.*

See below . . .

Ezekiel 32:24

*"There is Elam and all her multitude, All around her grave, **All of them slain, fallen by the sword, Who have gone down uncircumcised to the lower parts of the earth**, Who caused their terror in the land of the living; Now they bear their shame with those who go down to the Pit.*

This is one tricky scripture. Try reading it by leaving out the highlighted portion. Now who do you think Elam and all her multitude are? Demons? Demons cannot be slain by the sword but their human hosts can. In this prophecy, the human hosts are dead and the demons are in *Tartarus* . . . The pit.

Hosea 13:14

"I will ransom them from the power of the grave; I will redeem them from death. O Death, I will be your plagues! O Grave, I will be your destruction! Pity is hidden from My eyes.

Another reference to "The Last Great Day". Jesus Christ was and is the answer to sin and death.

Nahum 1:14

The Lord has given a command concerning you: "Your name shall be perpetuated no longer. Out of the house of your gods I will cut off the carved image and the molded image. I will dig your grave, For you are vile."

Clearly, this refers to a physical death sentence.

We complete this study on the hell doctrine by looking at two scriptures that are casually referred to as proof of the traditional teachings on heaven and hell. I hope all my readers will, in future, be a lot more diligent about checking the scriptures before accepting human reasoning when it comes to any issue in the Bible. Remember, there are no errors or contradictions in the Bible; only in human reasoning that has been corrupted by deception.

Thief on the Cross

The "**Thief on the Cross**" theory is a justification used to prove the validity of "**death-bed conversions**". This came about all for the want of a mis-placed comma. Please see for yourself and note that many other scriptures disprove this assumption . . .

Matthew 27

> [38]Then two robbers were crucified with Him, one on the right and another on the left.
> [39]And those who passed by blasphemed Him, wagging their heads
> [40]and saying, "You who destroy the temple and build it in three days, save Yourself! If You are the Son of God, come down from the cross."
> [41]Likewise the chief priests also, mocking with the scribes and elders, said,
> [42]"He saved others; Himself He cannot save. If He is the King of Israel, let Him now come down from the cross, and we will believe Him.
> [43]He trusted in God; let Him deliver Him now if He will have Him; for He said, 'I am the Son of God.' "
> [44]Even the robbers who were crucified with Him reviled Him with the same thing.

Mark 15

> [27]With Him they also crucified two robbers, one on His right and the other on His left.
> [28]So the Scripture was fulfilled which says, "And He was numbered with the transgressors."
> [29]And those who passed by blasphemed Him, wagging their heads and saying, "Aha! You who destroy the temple and build it in three days,

30save Yourself, and come down from the cross!"

31Likewise the chief priests also, mocking among themselves with the scribes, said, "He saved others; Himself He cannot save.

32Let the Christ, the King of Israel, descend now from the cross, that we may see and believe." Even those who were crucified with Him reviled Him.

Luke 23

39Then one of the criminals who were hanged blasphemed Him, saying, "If You are the Christ, save Yourself and us."

40But the other, answering, rebuked him, saying, "Do you not even fear God, seeing you are under the same condemnation?

41And we indeed justly, for we receive the due reward of our deeds; but this Man has done nothing wrong."

42Then he said to Jesus, "Lord, remember me when You come into Your kingdom."

43And Jesus said to him, "Assuredly, I say to you, today you will be with Me in Paradise."

How can we build a doctrine on one comma? Take away one comma and the doctrine falls apart: "I say to you today, you will be with me in paradise" or an Eden-like existence. This will happen at The Great White Throne Judgement of the Last Great Day.

The thief didn't fulfill the conversion process as identified in so many other parts of scripture. Also, we are told that **Jesus went to the grave that day, not into paradise**, and was held there for three days until He was resurrected and He hadn't yet returned to The Father.

This misunderstanding has given rise to so-called death-bed conversions which undermines the truth of God's word and creates contradictions. Jesus and the two robbers all went to the same place; the grave. **The robbers still sleep, but Christ is risen**.

Absent From the Body

"To be absent from the body is to be with the Lord"

This statement is trotted out to "prove" that Christians go straight to heaven after death. So read the following context for yourselves which disproves this assumption . . .

2 Corinthians 4

> *⁷But we have this treasure in earthen vessels, that the excellence of the power may be of God and not of us.*
> *⁸We are hard pressed on every side, yet not crushed; we are perplexed, but not in despair;*
> *⁹persecuted, but not forsaken; struck down, but not destroyed--*
> *¹⁰always carrying about in the body the dying of the Lord Jesus, that the life of Jesus also may be manifested in our body.*
> *¹¹For we who live are always delivered to death for Jesus' sake, that the life of Jesus also may be manifested in our mortal flesh.*
> *¹²So then death is working in us, but life in you.*
> *¹³And since we have the same spirit of faith, according to what is written, "I believed and therefore I spoke," we also believe and therefore speak,*
> *¹⁴knowing that He who raised up the Lord Jesus will also raise us up with Jesus, and will present us with you.*
> *¹⁵For all things are for your sakes, that grace, having spread through the many, may cause thanksgiving to abound to the glory of God.*
> *¹⁶Therefore we do not lose heart. Even though our outward man is perishing, yet the inward man is being renewed day by day.*
> *¹⁷For our light affliction, which is but for a moment, is working for us a far more*

exceeding and eternal weight of glory,

[18]while we do not look at the things which are seen, but at the things which are not seen. For the things which are seen are temporary, but the things which are not seen are eternal.

2 Corinthians 5

[1]For we know that if our earthly house, this tent, is destroyed, we have a building from God, a house not made with hands, eternal in the heavens.

[2]For in this we groan, earnestly desiring to be clothed with our habitation which is from heaven,

[3]if indeed, having been clothed, we shall not be found naked.

[4]For we who are in this tent groan, being burdened, not because we want to be unclothed, but further clothed, that mortality may be swallowed up by life.

[5]Now He who has prepared us for this very thing is God, who also has given us the Spirit as a guarantee.

[6]So we are always confident, **knowing that while we are at home in the body we are absent from the Lord.**

[7]For we walk by faith, not by sight.

[8]We are confident, yes, well pleased rather **to be absent from the body and to be present with the Lord.**

[9]Therefore we make it our aim, whether present or absent, to be well pleasing to Him.

Paul often spoke of the conflict of desire to stay and complete his work for Christ, or leave this mortal life and go on into eternity. This is confirmed in **Philippians Chapter One.**

Question is, where is Paul now? He is sleeping and has no concept of passing time. His very next moment of consciousness will be when he rises with the rest of the Christians at the time of the so-called Rapture. For him and all other dead Christians, that moment will be instantaneous.

No one, I repeat no one has preceded us into the kingdom of heaven.

The Christian Church Died in 1998

It was an act of global suicide for the Christian Church. Two hard-working UK Christian lay ministers were answering children's questions at their usual Sunday School meeting when the subject of Princess Diana was raised. The first anniversary of her death was coming up and they were addressing the question of whether she was in Heaven or Hell.

The men were emphatic in their assertion that, according to traditional evangelical teaching, Diana was now in hell.

The children went home and told their parents. The parents, apoplectic with fury and outrage, contacted the media and the public response matched the mood of the parents. The news went global and the entire Christian Church was put on the defensive. There was no unity, just a hodge-podge of half-hearted support or outright condemnation depending on which denomination was speaking.

The traditional Christian Church had already been under severe strains for its support of other doctrines that could not withstand close scrutiny, but this event was the last straw for many people.

It's one thing to stand up and fight for truth and justice when the cause is clearly defined and thoroughly endorsed by scripture, sound science and real-life experience; but quite another when the cause is muddled, contradictory, confused and archaic.

Many churches and teachers now play it safe and choose not to mention hell at all. This book, among others, will hopefully change that position and greatly enlighten not just the Church but the multitudes of people who have deserted the faith because of these aberrations.

How Much Time Do We Have Left?

A lot of prophecies are tied to what happens with Jerusalem. The modern State of Israel recaptured Jerusalem in the 6 day war called Yom Kippur in 1967. Prophecy scholars broadly agree that this was a pivotal event that started a count-down. The length of time of the countdown has been established as a maximum of 70 years. This is based on the statement that THIS GENERATION (the generation that saw the recapture of Jerusalem) will not pass away before Christ returns. The Biblical definition of a generation is 70 years as being the life-span of a normal life. This brings us to a maximum date of 2037. But I emphasize the word: Maximum. The fact is, Christ could return at any time between now and 2037. So we cannot afford to be complacent.

One Of The Surest Signs That The Return Of Jesus Christ Is Imminent, Is How Close We Are To Completing The Great Commission.

How will we know when the Great Commission has been completed?

This gospel shall be preached as a witness to all the nations . . . and then shall the end come. (**Matthew 24v14**)

The Two Witnesses? The Bible reveals who they are: (**Isaiah 43v10, Acts 1v8**)

The FIRST WITNESS was the Nation of Israel under the Old Covenant and the Law. THE LAW AND THE PROPHETS. (**Galatians 3v24**)

The SECOND WITNESS is the Church of Jesus Christ under the New Covenant and Grace.

Put more succinctly, the World needs BOTH WITNESSES: LAW and GRACE. (**Luke 16v16, Matthew 5v17-20**)

The Bible testifies to both. The gospel is tied up in both witnesses, so the Great Commission will be completed when **the Old and New Testament is made available in every language and nation of the world**.

Another major sign that Christ's return is imminent is THE GREAT FALLING AWAY (**2 Thessalonians 2v1-12**). A microcosm of this event took place in the life of Jesus (**John 6v60-69**) when He was deserted by ALL His followers except for the 12 disciples. This is prophesied to happen again, but on a global scale, when millions will desert the Church to embrace the new global religion which is presently being assembled. (Further reading @ www.endtimepilgrim.org/apostasy). All Christians can avoid this by being assured that ONLY the Bible is the Word of God and ONLY Christ is the way to salvation and ONLY living by His Word can we be certain of staying the course and growing in wisdom and knowledge.

EXPOSING
the Curse

*What Science, Religion and Politics have not
been able to tell you about*

LIFE, HEALTH, SEX and DEATH

and how this affects the debate on:

ABORTION, HOMOSEXUALITY
and END-OF-LIFE ISSUES

There is a curse that affects the lives of ALL human beings, that is as real as the law of gravity. Its effects are clearly seen in our day-to-day lives and soundly proven by legitimate scientific research and Biblical teaching.

Exposing The Curse identifies where all our problems come from and the ideal solutions to resolve them. We are all aware of national laws that govern our lives but few people are aware of the Planet-wide laws that impact our lives and the lives of our loved ones.

Knowledge is power and this information will help the reader make some very wise choices that will positively affect their future . . .

For more information,
visit our website at: www.exposingthecurse.com